DIRK STICHWEH

PHOTOGRAPHY BY JÖRG MACHIRUS AND SCOTT MURPHY

NEW YORK SKYSCRAPERS

PRESTEL

MUNICH BERLIN LONDON NEW YORK

TABLE OF CONTENTS

FOREWORD

New York City—a metropolis with a population of more than 8 million on the east coast of the United States—is not only home to the world's largest stock exchange and one of the major sources of the latest fashion and cultural trends but is also a media capital and the center of the entertainment industry. As a gateway to the New World, the city is a giant melting pot for people from all over the world. But New York City—generally known as New York for short—is also associated first and foremost with another distinctive feature, namely skyscrapers. Although Chicago can claim to be the birthplace of the genre, New York is considered synonymous with this archetypal American form of architecture.

After Chicago created the skyscraper type at the end of the 19ᵗʰ century with the buildings of the Chicago School, New York generally led the way right up to the postmodernist structures around 100 years later. New York was where all the important developments in the history of skyscrapers took place. While both cities were the places where new styles were invented, implemented, and launched, time and again New York building was a vital trendsetter that left its mark on international architectural history. Even within the headline-grabbing category of tallest building in the world, New York maintained its exceptional position over a long period. From the end of the 19ᵗʰ century until the 1970s, eight of the buildings constructed in New York alone could claim this prestigious title in uninterrupted succession.

The form, size, and height of skyscrapers were influenced by various factors over the decades. Initially the limitations were of a technical nature, but later zoning ordinances or even direct restrictions on height became critical factors. New developments and the growing ambitions of architects and their clients continued to influence interior and exterior design. With time and in-

Downtown skyline from around 1940

Skyline of Midtown Manhattan

creasing building heights, the achievements of structural engineers became of paramount importance.

With their combination of technology and aesthetics, skyscrapers constitute symbols of prestige and economic power. Not infrequently, they represent a statement by a multinational corporation, city, and sometimes even a whole country. That the construction of skyscrapers has, however, sometimes also been vehemently opposed is frequently the result of a lack of imaginative city planning. This was one reason why in New York during the 1960s the scale of entire areas was destroyed by the construction of anonymous concrete and glass boxes. Another mistake followed around two decades later when some streets were allowed too dense a concentration of skyscrapers during the building boom of the 1980s.

Frank Lloyd Wright, one of America's outstanding 20th-century architects, rejected the clustering of skyscrapers in business areas because he felt it diminished the importance of each individual building. However, the typical New York silhouette of the early 1930s, with a few dominant and outstanding towers, now belongs to the past. These days, what the viewer sees is a dense accumulation of structures from different stylistic periods. Despite all the criticism about excessive development, New York is still a brilliant example of how a large aggregation of skyscrapers can also have a soothing effect on the viewer. Because of the dialogue with other buildings, each one of them profits from the success of the others.

New York Skyscrapers describes the city's most significant high-rises, exploring their history and the influence that they have had on the urban landscape and urban development. In order to be able to better situate individual buildings in their historical context, the book begins with a brief history of skyscrapers. In the last 12 decades, there have been so many different developments and styles that a separate introduction would be needed to acknowledge all of them. Inevitably, the consequences of the devastating terrorist attacks on the World Trade Center (page 54), on September 11, 2001, must also be considered in terms of the history of high-rise construction in New York. This unparalleled act of violence not only dramatically altered the city's skyline but also influenced New Yorkers' sense of security, particularly of those involved in the construction of skyscrapers.

THE HISTORY OF SKYSCRAPERS

THE CHICAGO SCHOOL

In October 1871 a huge fire destroyed large parts of the city center of Chicago. Combined with the increasing importance of Chicago as a national hub of commerce and transportation of goods, this disaster paved the way for a completely new type of building. Although the first buildings after the conflagration were still built in the old style, they were different from their predecessors to the extent that their steel girders were clad with fireproof materials such as face brick. Over the following years, less and less value was placed on old traditions during the reconstruction of the city. As a result the skyscraper was born in Chicago.

Louis Sullivan (1856–1924)

At the end of the 19th century the most highly regarded architects of the period were at work in this city on the shores of Lake Michigan. The architects included not only in the founding father and probably greatest theoretician of high-rise buildings, Louis Sullivan, but also John Wellborn Root, Daniel Burnham, Frank Lloyd Wright, Dankmar Adler, William Holabird, and Martin Roche. They all had faith in the spirit of the age, and were convinced new technology in high-rise buildings would also generate new architecture. For them, the vertical emphasis of the buildings and the tripartite division of the facade—into base, shaft, and capital—was of extraordinary importance. The ideas of these architects became known collectively as the Chicago School of architecture, or Chicago School for short, and they formed the first major style in the history of skyscrapers.

By the century's end the size of plots of land in the city centers of New York and Chicago was becoming so cramped that building upward was the only way to solve the space problem. Hastening this development was the emergence of gridded streets, plus the fact that initially there were no firm building regulations or limitations on height. The move toward taller buildings was boosted by two major new technological developments. One of these was the invention of the elevator by Elisha Graves Otis in the mid-19th century. Elevators had already been installed in the first New York buildings as early as around 1870, so that all floors could be equally accessed. The second and almost even more important development was that of the steel-frame structure. Technically, this feature was indispensable for the construction of taller buildings, for the steel frame possessed a load-bearing capacity much greater than that of masonry.

Home Insurance Building, Chicago

The first skyscraper is generally acknowledged to be the Home Insurance Building by William LeBaron Jenney, constructed in Chicago in 1885. This was the first example of a high-rise building with a skeleton frame using structural steel. The weight was distributed onto pillars instead of onto the exterior masonry walls. Many critics, however, regard its designation as the first skyscraper as highly debatable, as it did not lead to progress nor did its emphasis lie in verticality. But rather the notable feature of the Home Insurance Building is its horizontal strips of masonry. It also did not feature riveted iron and steel frames unlike the Tacoma Building by Holabird and Roche, completed in 1889 a few yards to the north.

The Chicago School reached its peak between 1890 and 1900. Its architects used the cladding of the facade not to mask the structure lying behind it but in order to emphasize it. During this period, Chicago's leading role in high-rise construction became more and more evident. The first skyscrapers were generally 160 to 230 feet high and were constructed within the Chicago Loop. They formed a connected overall system that created many of the most important buildings of this formative period of skyscraper development. In general, with all these buildings, the prevailing principle was the decoration of structure and not the structure of decoration, as was preferred in distant New York.

New York Neoclassicism and the First Building Regulations

As in Chicago, soaring land prices in New York also attracted investors like a magnet. The first New York skyscrapers were constructed at the southern tip of Manhattan. In contrast to the Chicago tradition of uniform flat roofs, New York offered room for various styles and philosophies that followed no clear line. Not infrequently, these were towers overladen with historicist touches. It was the theatrical version of the skyscraper that was preferred here, and despite the drive for height there seemed to be little interest in taking advantage of technological innovation. Eyes were oriented more toward Europe and reproducing styles from the Old World. Only in 1889—four years after the Home Insurance Building in Chicago—did the Tower Building give New York its first steel-frame structure. The first skyscrapers still blended into the urban context. Though they were higher than the existing buildings, they were not so high as to enjoy unlimited domination of the skyline. Thus until 1890, Trinity Church at 281 feet was still the tallest building in the city.

With the passing of the first height-restriction ordinance in Chicago, limiting building heights to 130 feet, around the turn of the century, New York surged ahead as the leading center of high-rise building. The Chicago School was succeeded by the solemnity of Beaux-Arts neoclassicism. Many critics spoke of a degeneration into a dull architecture based on style, in which historical forms were slapped onto modern structures. In contrast to the buildings in Chicago, New York skyscrapers were not only considerably higher but also, because of their extraordinary shapes, much more spectacular. Thus the construction of the Flatiron Building (page 66) in 1902 attracted greater public interest than any previous new skyscraper structure. Together with the Singer Building (page 63), it was the godfather of all heavily ornamented skyscrapers constructed in Manhattan at the beginning of the 20th century. Yet the most important work of this period was the Woolworth Building (page 48), completed in 1913, which with a height of 792 feet would remain the tallest building in the world for 17 years.

In the first two decades of the 20th century, a more and more common phenomenon in downtown Manhattan was for high-rise buildings, constructed only a few years earlier, to be torn down to make way for even larger structures. These new high-rise office buildings had considerably larger ground plans and were as a result substantially more functionally efficient. In contrast to slender towers in which a relatively large space was lost to elevators and supply ducts, these new buildings had a better functional ratio. They frequently occupied a whole block, and sometimes had 20 to 30 stories. Until the building of these first large office boxes, the incidence of sunlight had been something that had always been taken for granted. In the narrow canyons of the streets around Wall Street, the incidence of natural light decreased with each new building, so that in almost all office buildings, even on a sunny day, artificial lighting was necessary at midday.

Flatiron Building, New York

With the construction of the Equitable Building (page 18) in 1915, it became clear even to opponents of building limitations that regulation of building was necessary in Manhattan. With more floor space than any other structure in the world at that date, the Equitable Building rose in a straight line through 36 stories, casting long shadows on surrounding streets. After many public hearings, the days of laissez-faire were over with the passing of New York's first land-use ordinance, known as the New York Zoning Law. A principal point in the ordinance—a milestone in the history of urban development—was a restriction on the distribution of mass. Henceforth, buildings could occupy the entire site only on the lower stories, depending on the width of the street. Above that, they had to be set back. If the building occupied only a quarter of the site, there were no restrictions on the tower's height. As a result of this first New York zoning ordinance, a new generation of skyscrapers took shape that would fundamentally alter the urban landscape during the following decades.

The Chicago Tribune Tower Competition and New York's Setback Skyscrapers
In the years immediately after World War I there was little in the way of high-rise building occurring in New York or any other North American metropolis. It was not until 1922, with the competition for the design of the Chicago Tribune Tower, that this situation would change, and it did so virtually overnight. The public competition for the headquarters of Chicago's largest daily newspaper, the *Chicago Tribune,* turned out to be one of the greatest architectural events of the 20th century. Attracted by a $50,000 prize and the opportunity to be able to design a prestigious high-rise building for Chicago's city center, more than 260 architects from all over the world took part in the competition.

All conceivable styles were represented, from ornate neoclassicism to the unadorned Bauhaus style of Walter Gropius. The commission was given to the architectural firm of Raymond Hood and John Mead Howells for a Gothic design complete with flying buttresses. However, many critics felt that the real winner of the competition was runner-up Eliel Saarinen. His design for an axial tower, soaring upward like a huge mountain mass, effortlessly seemed to overcome the gap between neoclassicism and modernism. In the years that followed, many new building projects in Chicago, New York, and other North American cities were strongly influenced in their arrangement of masses by Saarinen's model.

The skyscrapers built in New York in the 1920s were subject to the zoning law of 1916, and often came to look like sculptural mountains, where shape was more important than historical detail or stylistic orientation. The charcoal drawings of Hugh Ferriss at the beginning of the decade, which depicted high-rise buildings as mountain ranges of various shapes, served as models for many New York skyscrapers. The latter differed from existing buildings in that the distribution of massing was tiered, in what came to be known as setback skyscrapers. These often took on the appearance of terrace-like, stepped mountains. There had been setback buildings of this kind before, but now they were codified and required by law for buildings of any significant height.

The Golden Years
In 1925 the great showcase for the Art Deco style—Exposition Internationale des Arts Décoratifs et Industriels Modernes—took place in Paris. The fashion for streamlined shapes with ornamentation of silver gleaming stainless steel promoted here would have a substantial influence on American high-rise buildings at the end of the decade. Although Art Deco was subsequently often ignored by art historians, its ornamental effects are evident in some of the most imposing skyscrapers in New York. In contrast to the flat roofs of the Chicago School, the crowns of high-rise buildings from this period often look like exaggerated exclamation points.

With the economic boom of the late 1920s, a substantial number of skyscrapers were built in New York and these exhibited a more mature or refined style than their predecessors. They were elegant, tall, well-proportioned, and often lavishly ornamented. It was the most fruitful period of skyscraper building since the early years in Chicago. With a flourishing economy and building

Woolworth Building, New York

Tribune Tower, Chicago

Manhattan 1930: Buildings along 42nd Street

Chrysler Building, New York

activity to match, land prices in the business centers likewise soared into the stratosphere. This circumstance in itself forced developers to strive for even greater heights. Between 1929 and 1932, New York's skyline would be fundamentally altered. Many of the skyscrapers that are still notable today were completed within this short period. In addition, the focus of new building moved from the already densely built Financial District into the areas of midtown Manhattan. A distinctive cluster of high-rises sprang up along 42nd Street.

In 1930 height was the uncontested priority for new construction. The Woolworth Building had been the tallest building in the world for more than 17 years, and in New York bitter rivalry now broke out to wrest away this prestigious designation, with the leading contenders being the Bank of Manhattan Building on Wall Street (page 24), the Chrysler Building on 42nd Street (page 88), and the Empire State Building on Fifth Avenue (page 74). After William Van Alen's Chrysler Building had snatched the title from Van Alen's former partner H. Craig Severance and his Bank of Manhattan Building in spectacular fashion (Van Alen had the spire of the Chrysler Building constructed inside the building, out of sight), the rivalry ended in 1931, just one year later, with the completion of the Empire State Building.

When the 1,046-foot Chrysler Building opened its doors in 1930, it not only outranked every other building in the world but it also deprived the Eiffel Tower in Paris of the distinction of being the tallest structure ever built by human hand. More than any other building, the Chrysler Building also exemplified the perfect realization of the Art Deco style. The Empire State Building, completed the following year, was 1,250 feet high—more than 200 feet higher than the Chrysler Building. But it also set new standards in all other categories: especially remarkable was the rapid construction period of 13 months, which even by today's standards is a superb achievement of planning and engineering.

In the mid-1930s, there were more skyscrapers in New York than in the whole rest of the world. 18 of the 20 highest buildings were located here. Admittedly, the new, substantially higher structures did bring technical problems with them. For example, as height increased, wind pressure became an ever-greater problem that could only be offset by installing additional load-bearing elements which directed the wind force to the ground level. Another major problem that developed was the amount of space taken up by elevator shafts. Sometimes such technical issues could have also lead to a restriction in height.

The Wall Street crash of October 1929 hit the American economy when the construction boom was at its zenith; it would have dramatic consequences for the North American construction industry. When the full effects of the Great Depression were being felt in 1932, hardly any new building projects were undertaken and the oversupply of office space left many newly built skyscrapers empty. Even the Empire State Building was affected—its low occupancy rate, shortly after its opening, caused it to become popularly known as the "Empty State Building."

Around 1930, the style of skyscrapers began to undergo transformation, leading to a stronger emphasis on horizontals and an abandonment of the romantic of Art Deco forms. At the same time that the Chrysler Building was being inaugurated, just a few yards east, work was underway on the rather nondescript Daily News Building (page 92), which represented an entirely new style that looked toward the future. It was the first skyscraper that in form and detail can already be considered modernist. The architect responsible was Raymond Hood, who a few years earlier had created a final paean to neoclassicism with his design for the Chicago Tribune Tower. Just as Louis Sullivan represented the spirit of the Chicago School, Raymond Hood's buildings were a symbol of the change from neoclassicism via Art Deco to European modernism. As a leading architect, a short time later he was also involved in the construction of Rockefeller Center (page 150). This large-scale building project brought together the various tendencies that had surfaced in the 1920s and 1930s. The concept of Rockefeller Center as a city within a city, in which several skyscrapers were conceived in the context of their neighbors, set completely new standards. Construction on the project lasted from 1932 to 1940, dominating building activity in New York during the decade of the 1930s, and providing an endpoint for the era of pre–World War II skyscraper construction.

Modernism Conquers North America

Perhaps no style of skyscraper architecture is so closely associated with one name, as modernism is with Ludwig Mies van der Rohe. The German-born architect produced his first design for a completely glazed high-rise in Berlin in 1922, but construction was not deemed feasible at that time. Later he became director of the Bauhaus in Dessau. In 1937 Mies emigrated to the United States to become the head of the School of Architecture at, what is now, the Illinois Institute of Technology in Chicago. It was here that modernism would flourish, becoming responsible for fundamentally changing the appearance of American cities. However, the beginning of the modernist age in the United States can be dated to as early as 1932 when the exposition "Modern Architecture: International Exhibition," conceived by Henry-Russell Hitchcock and Philip Johnson, was shown at the Museum of Modern Art. The catalogue that accompanied this exhibition was called *The International Style*—the American term for Bauhaus modernism. The same year, William Lescaze's Philadelphia Savings Fund Society Building presented the first combination of the reductive style of the early Chicago School with its steel-frame structure, and the metal and glass structures of modernism (along with the McGraw-Hill Building in New York, it was the only high-rise to be mentioned in Johnson and Hitchcock's pioneering exhibition). The new style achieved its final breakthrough 20 years later, however, as in the late 1930s and the following decade building activity was minimal or insignificant.

After World War II, architects found themselves at a crossroads. Classical architecture and Art Deco were no longer options as styles. It was a time of pragmatism and economy. Neither the craftsmen nor the money was available for lavish ornamentation. Buildings were increasingly produced industrially and underwent a degree of standardization. The formula consisted of

Empire State Building, New York

new materials, simple forms, and austere, undecorated exterior surfaces. Mies's idea of skin-and-bones architecture envisaged surfaces that were as transparent as possible. Facades were replaced by curtain walls, a curtain of glazing enclosing buildings within an exterior wall consisting of windows and stainless-steel frames, which is one of the most conspicuous features of the International Style. The first completely glass-clad residential building in the United States was Mies's Lakeshore Drive Apartments in Chicago, built in 1951. These boxy glass structures seemed, during the postwar period, to be the only appropriate direction for architecture. They were cheap and could be used for virtually any type of building. The glass box thus became the trademark of the 1950s and 1960s.

After World War II skyscraper construction was slow to get started again. As noted, because the pre-Depression construction boom had left an overabundance of unused office space, only around 1950 did demand begin again and work resume on the construction of new skyscrapers. From 1947 to 1960, the preferred types of skyscraper in New York were the bulky type with a truncated tower or the tall box shape with no setbacks. Only 20 of the 109 new buildings completed during this period had more than 30 floors. The classic tripartite division was almost completely dispensed with. The rather stocky-looking buildings also lacked the stylishness of prewar structures, but on the other hand they were considerably more rentable and spacious. Because of the latest technological developments, the usable proportion grew from 65–70 percent to 80 percent of gross floor area in the large, fully air-conditioned offices.

Along with many unimportant new buildings, construction in New York in the 1950s produced those skyscrapers that can be considered milestones of classic modernism. These include the Secretariat Building of the United Nations (page 94), completed in 1952, which was the first office tower to feature a curtain wall. However, its slender north and south facades are still clad with marble elements. The new standards were implemented in their entirety shortly after, in the construction of Lever House on Park Avenue (page 128). This building, only 302 feet high, is totally enclosed in a glass skin. In its provision of public space, it also brought more light into the densely built streets of Manhattan.

The culmination of modernism was the Seagram Building in New York (page 124), designed by Mies van der Rohe and Philip Johnson. Completed in 1958, this office building combines all the positive qualities of the International Style, and in its attention to detail remains a unique work of art. Unfortunately, the Seagram Building did not offer scope for further development, unlike earlier styles. The logical outcome of this was countless imitations that possessed neither its degree of originality nor its love of detail. The principle of "less is more" was taken by imitators as a challenge to produce anonymous glass boxes as a kind of mass product lacking all emotional appeal. These often bland glass grid containers looked as if they had been made of prefabricated elements, and were a crucial element in the discrediting of modernist skyscraper architecture.

PUBLIC SPACE AND NEW RECORD BUILDINGS

New York City officials were so impressed with the design of the Seagram Building and its provision for public space that shortly after they revised the old building regulations. The resulting zoning ordinance was an extensive revision of the 1916 version. A basic difference lay in the greater attention paid to total floor area relative to the size of the plot. The floor space index ratio of a skyscraper was not allowed to be more than 15 times greater than the site area. (In comparison, at the beginning of the century it was occasionally more than 30 times as much.) If provision was made for public space, the value could be increased by 20 percent.

Because of the new restrictions, box-shaped buildings clearly brought in the greatest profit, and consequently were the preferred type of structure thereafter. The additional policy of transferring "packages" of air rights from one building to another or combining those of several buildings was seen as an invitation for many unsavory deals. Air rights were now bartered, opening

Rockefeller Center, New York

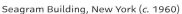

Seagram Building, New York (c. 1960)

the way for collections of anonymous office boxes made of steel, concrete, and glass, which shot up without any regard for the urban fabric.

However, in the mid-1960s the first signs of new styles in skyscraper building could be found. These structures did not differ fundamentally from the International Style office blocks—proof that modernism had not yet died. The Marina City Towers on the Chicago River were among the first skyscrapers to break with the angular shape that had defined modernism. Their rounded concrete towers, resembling corncobs, quite deliberately constituted a contrast with the right angles of modernism. A further sign came with Eero Saarinen's CBS Building in New York (page 154). His emphasis on verticality was the first indication of a rejection of the prevailing horizontal style. The CBS Building provided a pleasant change in this section of the Avenue of the Americas (Sixth Avenue), which in the 1960s and 1970s had mutated into a densely built corridor of uniformly designed office towers between 42nd and 55th Street that no longer allowed any connection with life on the street to develop. The "modernist box" is now considered an aesthetic cul-de-sac that permitted no place for variation or new ideas. As Philip Johnson, one of the founders and great champions of the International Style, wearily commented at the end of the 1960s: "Modern architecture has turned out to be a flop. Cities are uglier than they were 50 years ago."

Late modernist skyscrapers can be regarded as a logical continuation of early modernism. In them, modernism is liberated from the confines of its self-imposed dogmatism. The transition to late modernism cannot be attributed to any single structure or to a particular year. There was no event or new movement that could have led to a radical change. It was in fact a slow process of mutation. At the end of the 1960s, it was mainly Chicago's skyscrapers that embodied a relaxation of the strict modernist framework. Lake Point Tower on Lake Michigan, for example, a cloverleaf-shaped building with a typical modernist curtain wall, broke with the rectangle in the curved lines of its floor plan.

The high-rise buildings of the late 1960s would distinguish themselves from their predecessors in their increased reliance on new technology, evidenced in new load-bearing structures, which would become a typical feature of these skyscrapers. In contrast to earlier buildings, the new buildings made use of exterior load-bearing elements and a central steel core. The new technology rendered the intrusive support elements on the interior largely superfluous, which at the same time provided a more efficient use of the available space. The visible diagonal and cross struts on the external walls of skyscrapers were at this time a trademark of the architectural firm Skidmore, Owings & Merrill. Its architects Bruce Graham and Gordon Bunshaft, in conjunction with the structural engineer Fazlur Khan, embodied the ethos and style of late modernism. The solution to late modernism's technical challenges found its aesthetic expression in the load-bearing structure. In these buildings, the cost of work and materials could be halved in comparison with the buildings of the 1920s and 1930s. Structures featuring the steel tube and cross-bracing structure that Skidmore, Owings & Merrill developed first attracted global attention in the late 1960s with the construction of the John Hancock Center in Chicago. At 1,127 feet high, it was at the time the second-highest building in the world after the Empire State Building.

In New York during the late 1960s and 1970s, the skyscrapers that were erected were mainly notable for their lack of imagination. The best examples of these are three almost identical extensions to Rockefeller Center on the Avenue of the Americas (XYZ buildings, page 158) and 55 Water Street at the southern tip of Manhattan (page 30). The latter, on its completion in 1972, stood as the largest office building in the world, with a gross floor area of 3.5 million square feet. The architect, the noted firm of Emery Roth & Sons, had an unmatched record at the time for designing large numbers of new buildings that permanently defined the urban scene as a kind of mass product.

In the 1960s, Emery Roth & Sons joined forces with architect Minoru Yamasaki in carrying out a new project that would eclipse all previous schemes: the World Trade Center. The Twin Towers of the World Trade Center (page 54) were the tallest and largest skyscrapers in the world when they were com-

John Hancock Center, Chicago

High-rises on the Avenue of the Americas, New York

World Trade Center in its urban context, New York

pleted in southern Manhattan in 1973. Every statistic represented a new superlative. With towers 1,368 and 1,362 feet high, they surpassed the Empire State Building by approximately 120 feet. Including all the ancillary buildings, they had a total floor space of over 10 million square feet. The exterior walls contained a dense array of vertical steel supports forming a lattice. The effect was of a self-contained rigid tube capable of carrying the weight of the building. The era of true record-high buildings reached an end a year later with the Sears Tower in Chicago. With a height of 1,454 feet, after 80 years it returned the title of tallest building in the world to the city that gave birth to skyscrapers, though without Chicago being able to shake off the stigma of being permanently second place.

Sears Tower, Chicago

This new and extremely tall generation of skyscrapers required new technology not only in terms of support systems. The configuration of elevator shafts also needed rethinking. The so-called "sky lobbies" were first installed in a skyscraper at the World Trade Center. This system of a kind of interchange station solved burgeoning planning problems and facilitated better use of large areas of floor space. Other buildings were provided with double-deck elevators that considerably reduced the amount of floor space required for elevator shafts.

In the second half of the 1970s, late modernist skyscrapers occasionally achieved sculptural qualities with their geometric floor plans. Philip Johnson's IDS Center in Minneapolis, for example, has an octagonal floor plan and is sliced up into facets at the angles. But the Citigroup Center in New York (page 104) with its slanted roof, or John Portman's cylindrical glass structures, such as his Western Peachtree Plaza in Atlanta, also embody the glamour of late modernism.

POSTMODERNISM OVERCOMES THE BOX

No exact date can be identified for the end of late modernism and the beginning of postmodernism. The transition phase that began in the mid-1970s and reached its conclusion at the beginning of the following decade was marked by a hodgepodge of buildings. Although the skyscrapers of the period wished to distance themselves from classic modernism, they were incapable of taking a major step forward to establish a new architectural style. Retrospectively, one might describe the high-tech structures of the 1970s as a constructive transition. The modernist box turned into sophisticated sculpture, but initially retained a distaste for facade art.

The great difference between postmodernism and the previous periods was that no longer did any one stylistic element have absolute authority. What was built instead was an agglomeration of pastiches. In contrast to the International Style, postmodernism manifested a strong affinity for design. A typical feature of postmodernist architecture is the pronounced return to masonry facades, and their ability to bring out the gradations, lines, and coloration of facades more than any other material. While these buildings meet the most up-to-date technological standards, they revel in traditional ornamentation. Advanced technical achievements were employed not to produce uniform products, but high-quality individual solutions. The principle of "anything goes" gave rise to a mix of arcades, pinnacles, turrets, pilasters, decorative gables, and color.

Synonymous with the designs of the postmodernist period is Philip Johnson, an architect who once more was one step ahead of the trend. Formerly one of the greatest champions of modernism, with the AT&T Building he created the most significant postmodernist structure anywhere, finally ensuring the permanent burial of modernism. The clear tripartite division of the building and its conspicuous pediment that resembled a Chippendale highboy meant that no one could fail to note the new characteristics and their difference from the style of the previous era.

In the postmodernist period, signature buildings became the rule. Whereas in the mid-1980s postmodern skyscrapers stood out by being different from neighboring buildings, with time architects became increasingly adept at fitting their new building projects seamlessly into their surroundings. Under the impression of a growing regional awareness, the importance of this aspect grew steadily. Postmodernist architecture achieved its greatest successes where it tied in with the style of the 1920s and 1930s and the technological achievements of modernism.

During the building boom of the 1980s, the popularity of skyscrapers spread from North America to other continents. Until then, few cities apart from New York and Chicago could boast of a respectable number of high-rise buildings. Today, skyscrapers are an accepted part of the urban landscape of many large cities all over the world. Along with a number of European metropolises, cities in East Asia in particular have seen spectacular new buildings spring up in great numbers during the past 25 years.

When the boom in new skyscrapers was at its height in East Asia and Europe, the North American construction industry was struck by recession. The demand for office space plummeted, and investment in real estate seemed like a bad prospect. In Manhattan alone, more than 375 million square feet of office space was available—double the amount in 1960. At the same time, architectural controversy broke out over the end of postmodernism and the beginning of a new modernism. The apologists for the latter demanded a new objectivity and a return to practical reasoning in architecture. Durability and constancy were to be the defense against the continually changing whims of fashion and consumer behavior. The skyscrapers built since the turn of the millennium can no longer be attributed to a particular style. They are frequently different from the previous generation in once again displaying features of classical modernism or reflecting elements of deconstructivism in their design.

Skyscrapers in the 21st Century

The new generation of extremely tall skyscrapers built in recent years, mainly in Asia, are based on a system of steel tubes filled with high-performance concrete. The tubes are linked with the central concrete core on several levels, enabling a substantial reduction in the movement of the structure at great height. Well-known examples of this new load-bearing structure are the Petronas Towers in Kuala Lumpur, the Jin Mao Tower in Shanghai, and the Taipei

AT&T Building, New York

101 Financial Center in Taiwan. Including its 200-foot mast, the latter has a total height of 1,667 feet, and since 2004 has claimed the coveted title of the tallest building in the world. Realistic schemes for skyscrapers exceeding the 1,500-foot mark are on the drawing board in cities all over the world. On the site of the former Twin Towers of the World Trade Center in New York, the Freedom Tower skyscraper is currently under construction. On its expected completion in 2011, this should reach a height of 1,776 feet. In the same year, Chicago is planning to pass the 2,000-foot mark with the Chicago Spire. However, neither building will be the tallest building in the world at that date: in Dubai the 180-story Burj Dubai will open its doors by the end of 2009. With its apex, this major project will reach a height of 2,658 feet and form the climax of the construction boom that has begun recently in the United Arab Emirates.

For other Asian cities, there are even sketches of vertical residential cities reaching a height of more than 3,300 feet and accommodating 100,000 people. However, at present, building projects of this kind are beyond existing technical capabilities. They are also not justifiable on economic grounds, since from the 100th floor upward, building costs begin to soar into the stratosphere. With heights of this kind, even with the latest innovative load-bearing structure, deflections due to markedly higher wind pressure can scarcely be coped with. A further disadvantage of extremely high structures is that they destroy the homogeneity of the existing skyline. In contrast with them, buildings that are 600 feet or so high look like dwarves. The visual interest in the skyline of New York (or any other metropolis) needs to be preserved in the future with buildings that fit the context in shape and height. Because of their exclusive design, even shorter buildings often achieve the great showpiece effect that viewers seek. The best examples of this are Rem Koolhaas's CCTV headquarters in Peking, which represented a completely new challenge in statics, and Norman Foster's Swiss Re headquarters in London, where the overall outline made it a new symbol of the city.

The horrific events of September 11, 2001, also gave people pause for thought about the sense and nonsense of huge skyscraper projects. When terrorists steered two commercial airliners into the Twin Towers of the World Trade Center in New York, causing them to collapse shortly after, not only politicians faced the great challenge of averting such attacks in the future. The terrorists' act—one that cost nearly 3,000 lives—prompted a reexamination of skyscraper construction. Not only do buildings of this kind offer a potential target for these attacks because of their prestigious nature, but also evacuating them is extremely complicated and has given many architects and their clients pause.

Skyscrapers of the 21st century must meet not only economic but also ecological criteria. To reduce energy consumption, today everyone involved in building high-rises must work together to plan and create new buildings. Facades are increasingly given over to high-performance glazing. Such climate-responsive facades make use of external conditions and use them as a source of energy in the form of sunshine and warmth. With today's "bioclimatic skyscrapers," manufacturers combine heat pumps, photovoltaic plants, and solar panels with each other, transforming high-rise buildings into mini-power stations. Along with the recently completed new buildings in New York such as the Hearst Tower (page 186) or the Bank of America Tower (page 172), the Commerzbank Tower in Frankfurt, Germany, built in 1997, represents one of the first and best examples of the implementation of an innovative building concept.

The Commerzbank Tower highlights the fact that, with 120 years of history behind them, skyscrapers have continued to develop from the theoretical beginnings of the Chicago School, through New York neoclassicism and Art Deco via modernism's rationality to the present-day style. These new designs feature various components borrowed from the extensive history of architectural form.

Commerzbank Tower, Frankfurt

Burj Dubai, Dubai

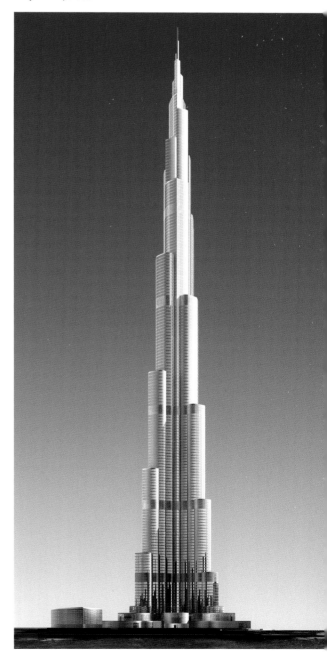

CHAPTER

THE FINANCIAL DISTRICT

The Financial District covers roughly the area that was once the earliest settlement of Manhattan. Today there remain very few of the historic buildings that reflect the original character of the district. Already by the beginning of the 20th century, the urban landscape was dominated by skyscrapers around Wall Street. Their slender towers gave the area a unique appearance. Two of the tallest and best-proportioned skyscrapers in the city are to be found here: the Trump Building (page 24) and the American International Building (page 34). At the beginning of the 1970s the land along the East River underwent major development that incorporated large, modern skyscrapers. These buildings even began to draw some attention away from Wall Street. The Financial District is best viewed from Brooklyn Bridge, from which it presents the city's most well-known face.

KEY

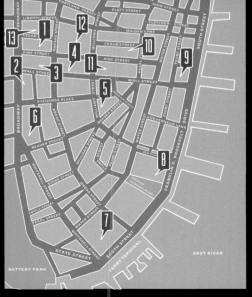

1 Equitable Building

2 Bank of New York Building

3 Bankers Trust Company Building

4 Trump Building

5 20 Exchange Place

6 Standard Oil Building

7 One New York Plaza

8 55 Water Street

9 120 Wall Street

10 American International Building

11 60 Wall Street

12 Chase Manhattan Bank Building

13 Marine Midland Bank Building

EQUITABLE BUILDING
(ALSO KNOWN AS 120 BROADWAY)

ADDRESS	STORIES	COMPLETION	HEIGHT	ARCHITECT
120 Broadway	36	1915	538 feet	Ernest R. Graham, of Graham, Anderson, Probst & White

When the Equitable Building was completed in 1915 after almost three years of construction, it generated considerable public outcry. Resembling a huge filing cabinet, the structure occupies a 165 x 300-foot site on lower Broadway previously the site of the old Equitable Building. Built in 1870, the latter was the first New York office building to include elevators. In 1912 it fell victim to a major fire. For the developer of the new Equitable Building, the industrialist Thomas Coleman Du Pont, it was a speculative scheme intended solely to turn a profit. It was also for this reason that for the first time in a skyscraper, the number of floors was adjusted to allow for optimal space for elevator and supply shafts. Following calculations by structural engineer Charles Knox, the number of floors was reduced from 40 to 36. With a gross floor area of more than 1.65 million square feet—equal to more than thirty times the size of the site—the Equitable Building constituted a new superlative and was only surpassed in 1931 by the Empire State Building (page 74).

above: Total view from the south-west side
below: Entrance portal on Broadway

The distinguished Chicago architectural firm of Graham, Anderson, Probst & White was commissioned to design the building. In Chicago, stricter building regulations should have precluded such a massive skyscraper on the site, as the Equitable Building was 50 percent larger than any other comparable building in the midwest. Inside, it was a kind of city within a city, with more than 13,000 employees working in an office area of 1.2 million square feet at peak times. Rising above the lobby's expansive vaulted coffered ceiling are the stacked identical floors. The building's facades have Renaissance Revival-style terra-cotta features, rising as two parallel masses without a setback. With their identical strips of windows, the facade creates a rather dull if nonetheless impressive image.

However, the Equitable Building's great importance for architectural history is not a factor of its capacity. The monstrous new edifice cast gigantic shadows on neighboring buildings in the densely built-up area. The adjacent streets were transformed into uninviting, gloomy canyons from which the stale air would not escape on a calm day. The effect is particularly noticeable at the corner of Pine Street and Broadway, where the traditional and markedly smaller American Surety Building (at 100 Broadway) is only about 10 yards away from the front of the Equitable Building. In all the other buildings in the immediate vicinity, operating costs increased because of the greater need for electric light. Their owners were noticeably worse off commercially since the newly available offices in the Equitable Building created a surplus of office space. As a result, the demand for greater regulation of skyscraper construction in New York became too loud to ignore, as calls came for an end to the rampant speculation. The furor surrounding the Equitable Building spurred the New York zoning ordinance that came into force just one year after the building was completed, and which aimed to prevent this kind of unchecked development. In 1996 the New York City Landmarks Preservation Commission nonetheless added the Equitable Building to its ranks of designated historic landmarks.

BANK OF NEW YORK BUILDING

(FORMERLY IRVING TRUST COMPANY BUILDING)

Aerial view

ADDRESS	STORIES	COMPLETION	HEIGHT	ARCHITECT
1 WALL STREET	50	1931	654 FEET	RALPH WALKER OF VOORHEES, GMELIN & WALKER

The Bank of New York Building was built in 1931 on what was said to be the most expensive piece of land in New York, located on the corner of Broadway and Wall Street. Measuring 180 x 115 square feet, the plot is adjacent to the New York Stock Exchange on the west, and cost more than $10 million, which was a record price at the time. (For comparison, the total building costs for the Empire State Building [page 74], constructed the same year at twice the height, came to $42 million.) The client for this new project was the New York Irving Trust Company, which up to then had had offices in the Woolworth Building (page 48). At the end of the 1920s, the bank's steady growth had prompted its management to seek a building of its own. The architect commissioned was the reputable Ralph Walker, who had a number of award-winning designs to his credit.

In this Art Deco skyscraper, the architect opted for a light-colored limestone facade with undulating east and west surfaces. Vertical strips of windows are placed inside the concave bays, which give the building a vertical profile and reinforce the impression of height. Standing at some distance, the viewer might be reminded of an oversize stone theater curtain. The massive base area occupies almost the entire site, rising to the 20th floor. Above that are several gently rounded setbacks that end in a slender tower. The massing conforms to the specifications of the New York Zoning Resolution of 1916. A three-story crown with a single large window on each side forms the top of the building. These windows permit daylight to illuminate the sumptuous mosaics in the conference rooms behind, and open up to offer a fantastic view of the Financial District from an elevation of about 650 feet.

At street level, the Bank of New York Building is distinguished by three-story Art Deco entrance portals. The large banking hall that lies beyond these doors is known as the *Red Room* because of its red terrazzo floor and the glowing red-patterned mosaics on the walls covering an area of 2,700 square feet. These mosaics, as well as the gold ceiling mosaics, are the work of the artist Hildreth Meière.

In 1987 the Irving Trust Company was taken over by the Bank of New York. At the same time the building with the prestigious address of 1 Wall Street also changed hands. 10 years later, the Bank of New York left its old premises at 48 Wall Street, moving to what would now become the Bank of New York Building. After the city had granted the building landmark status in March 2001, the owners began an extensive renovation of the facade surfaces, which has only recently been completed.

Entrance on Wall Street

BANKERS TRUST COMPANY BUILDING

ADDRESS	STORIES	COMPLETION	HEIGHT	ARCHITECT
14 WALL STREET	39	1912	539 FEET	TROWBRIDGE & LIVINGSTONE

In order to be able to erect the Bankers Trust Company Building on this prime location at the intersection of Wall and Nassau Street, the first thing that had to be done in 1910 was to demolish the Gillender Building, which had been constructed only 13 years earlier. At the time of its completion, the extremely slender 273-foot structure was among the tallest buildings in the city. Measured by the demands of the early 20th century, however, it made inadequate use of the space available. Two years after it was demolished, the Bankers Trust Company had completed its new office building on the site, which measured only 102 x 105 feet. At 539 feet, it was twice as high as its predecessor, and in its day the tallest bank building in the world. It was also the dominant feature of Wall Street, a dominance it lost during the construction boom of the late 1920s, when it was eclipsed by skyscrapers exceeding 600 feet.

Like so many other skyscrapers built in Manhattan in the early 20th century, the Bankers Trust Company Building also made use of historicizing elements. It thus blended seamlessly into a chain of skyscrapers that created the impression that American architecture was vying with the achievements of the Old World or trying to outdo them. The structure features the classic tripartite division in its elevation. Ionic columns are arranged around the four-story base, rising to a decorated cornice. Above this is a 20-story shaft, clad in a plain, light-gray granite. On each side are five vertical rows of paired windows.

As a pendant to the column in the lower part of the building, an array of Ionic columns forms a transition to the pyramidal capital. The prominent, distinctive shape of the latter was exploited by the bank inasmuch as it used the shape of the roof, which covered its archives as the company logo. Less than 20 years after its completion, two 25-story extensions were added to the office tower on the north and west sides. Although the new facades blended smoothly with the older part of the building, their general design was in line with the fashions of the early 1930s. The original tower is now a designated landmark.

With its colonnades on the lower part of the building, the Bankers Trust Company Building echoes Federal Hall, one block east. Built in 1842, Federal Hall is one of the finest neoclassical structures in the city. A statue of George Washington on its steps marks the place where Washington took oath as the first president of the United States on April 30, 1789. In his day, the building that stood on this site was the old City Hall (demolished in 1812), which from 1789 to 1790 was the seat of Congress during the brief period when New York was capital of the United States.

above: Aerial view from the east
below: Federal Hall with the George Washington Statue

TRUMP BUILDING

(FORMERLY BANK OF MANHATTAN BUILDING; 40 WALL STREET)

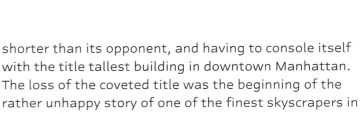

ADDRESS	STORIES	COMPLETION	HEIGHT	ARCHITECT
40 Wall Street	70	1930	927 feet	H. Craig Severance & Yasuo Matsui

The Bank of Manhattan Building (now the Trump Building) was among the building projects that vied for the title of tallest building in the world at the end of the 1920s. As a result of the economic boom and flourishing construction industry during this period, the existing title holder, the Woolworth Building (page 48), completed in 1913, was waiting to be knocked off its pedestal. Architects H. Craig Severance and Yasuo Matsui thought they could carry off the prestigious distinction with their 70-story design for an office building. When they learned, however, that William Van Alen was aiming for a height of 919 feet with the Chrysler Building (page 88), then under construction, outbidding their scheme by a few feet, they decided to extend their building. After the fact, they added a mast to the scheme, raising the height to 927 feet, so that for one month it was indeed the tallest building in the world. At that date, however, the two architects were not aware that Van Alen was having a 180-foot spire constructed inside the building, and this emerged from the roof after the rival building had opened. It left the Bank of Manhattan Building 120 feet

shorter than its opponent, and having to console itself with the title tallest building in downtown Manhattan. The loss of the coveted title was the beginning of the rather unhappy story of one of the finest skyscrapers in New York.

The story began in 1928, when seven smallish plots of land on Wall Street were bought and merged into a single site. Work started on construction shortly thereafter. Only 11 months were allowed for construction (expected to be a record), which required advance planning down to the smallest detail. In its lower section, the building has a symmetrical arrangement of setbacks, above which a slender tower structure rises. Above the shaft, the building culminates in a green patinated copper roof in a French Renaissance style. With its skylights, the roof forms a decidedly successful termination, ending in a no less elegant, ornate Gothic spire.

As a result of the Great Depression, up to the end of World War II only half the total floor area of 900,000 square feet found tenants. To make matters worse, in 1946 a Coast Guard plane crashed into the tower during foggy weather. The building only gained a profitable occupancy level with the boom of the early 1950s. After several changes of ownership, the investor Donald Trump acquired the rundown building in the mid-1990s for a mere $8 million, and began the thorough restoration of a building mightily in need of refurbishing. In the course of this work, all 3,500 windows were replaced and the two-story lobby was expensively clad with marble and gleaming bronze surfaces. Since the completion of the restoration, the building has been called the "crown jewel of Wall Street"—acknowledging its recaptured former glory. The original idea of dividing the top 35 floors into condominiums was rejected, as was the notion of reopening to the public the observation deck that had been freely accessible during the building's first two decades. Although the present building still ranks among the tallest in the city at the beginning of the 21st century, it has lost something of its impact as a result of the dense, high-rise development of its immediate surroundings. The position of the site within a block of buildings further reinforces this effect.

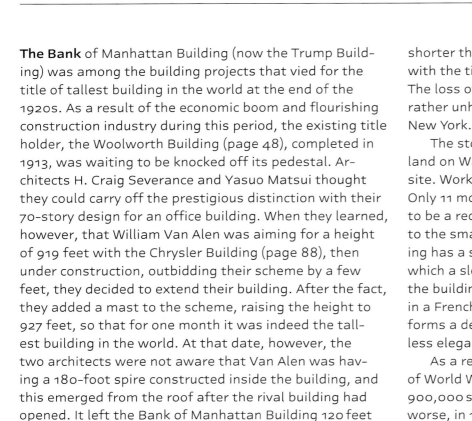

above: Detail near the top of the building
below: "Crown jewel of Wall Street"

20 EXCHANGE PLACE

(FORMERLY CITY BANK FARMERS TRUST COMPANY BUILDING)

ADDRESS	STORIES	COMPLETION	HEIGHT	ARCHITECT
20 EXCHANGE PLACE	55	1931	741 FEET	CROSS & CROSS

As a result of extensive construction during the late 1920s, the concentration of skyscrapers in the immediate vicinity of Wall Street had already reached a high density by around 1930. The few remaining plots that were suitable for high-rise buildings were generally so small that, given the existing building regulations and the sky-high land prices, no buildings could have been erected profitably. One of the few sites still available lay south of Wall Street on a trapezoidal piece of land at Exchange Place. In this case, a prestigious site in the direct vicinity of the Stock Exchange seemed to the clients more important than the muted impact that a slender tower—the only type of high-rise that could be built at this location—would have.

According to the original plans of 1929, this new building scheme had a proposed height of 919 feet, making it the tallest structure in the world. In contrast to the building's present form, in the original design the shaft was 130 feet longer and terminated in a pyramidal top. However, the effects of the Great Depression forced a change in plans for the upper part of the building, so that the tower finally reached a height of only 741 feet. In retrospect, even if the original plans had been implemented, the coveted title of tallest building would not have come its way since, at the time of its completion, buildings such as the Empire State Building (page 74) or the Chrysler Building (page 88) would have clearly outstripped it.

Now known as 20 Exchange Place, the skyscraper has a 15-story base clad in white Alabama limestone. At the transition to the slim tower, the central support pillars between the 15th and 18th floors terminate in three-story-high stone sculptures, whose decorative Egyptian head motifs conceal ventilation shafts. At this level, the parapet features are adorned with agricultural motifs and ornamentation in the shape of large coins. As a synonym for prosperity, these were intended to draw attention to the business divisions of City Bank Farmers Trust Company. The shaft is slightly rotated on its axis relative to the base. The profiled corners are clad in white limestone. The central areas between them with their rows of three paired windows are finished in brick, whose original light coloring has turned brownish as a result of years of pol-

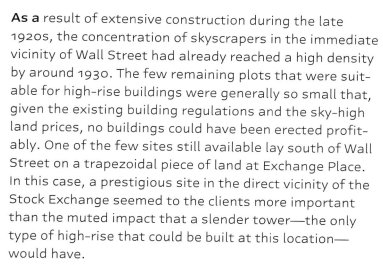

above: View from the south-west side
below: Facade decoration between the 15th and 18th floors

lution from passing traffic. The capital is characterized by three secondary setbacks. In its lower stories rows of paired windows terminate in decorated, three-storied round arches.

At street level, bronze doors with ornamental motifs related to agriculture and transportation provide access to the entrance lobby. The lobby is subtly illuminated and lavishly decorated, with multicolored marble features, mosaics, and a gold-colored travertine floor. The splendid rotunda lobby with its marble columns and the wood-paneled Senior Officers' Hall are no longer accessible to the public. The ceiling painting, *Allegory of Wealth and Beauty* by Hildreth Meière, was removed during the course of later renovation work. During a recent reconfiguration, the floors above the 15th story were converted into a residential wing with 350 apartments. The lower floors continue to be used as offices.

STANDARD OIL BUILDING

(ALSO KNOWN AS 26 BROADWAY)

ADDRESS	STORIES	COMPLETION	HEIGHT	ARCHITECT
26 BROADWAY	31	1922	518 FEET	CARRÈRE & HASTINGS

Total view of the building from the south

above: Entrance on Broadway
below: Symbol for a strong market:
The Charging Bull

Until the end of the 19th century, the Standard Oil Company almost monopolized the American oil market. Some 10 years after the Supreme Court broke up John D. Rockefeller's Standard Oil Trust Organization into numerous separate companies in 1911, the company's New York headquarters at the southern tip of Manhattan planned to expand. During World War I and the years immediately after there had been virtually no major building activity in New York of note. Only with the beginning of the new decade and the strengthening of the American economy into the greatest commercial and financial power in the world was there once again investment in major building projects. The Standard Oil Company of New York (Socony) decided to add floors to the building housing its headquarters on lower Broadway, which had been constructed in 1885.

With its curved facade following the line of lower Broadway, the design by the distinguished firm of Carrère and Hastings represents a good example of a building sensitive to its urban context. The monumental structure with its Renaissance Revival features fits harmoniously with the surrounding buildings, yet is distinguished from them. Because of its H-shaped ground plan, the 15-story base allows a sufficient supply of daylight into the office spaces that face the interior. A tower rises from the middle of the building, slightly rotated in relation to the base. Its upper three floors are graced with colonnades of Ionic columns, on top of which is a tiered pyramidal roof structure terminating in a large beacon, whose light was once visible even from the Port of New York (today that view is obscured by modern skyscrapers). Since 1989, near the main entrance of the Standard Oil Building has stood Arturo DeModica's bronze statue *The Charging Bull*—a symbol for bull stock markets, and a favorite subject of photographers.

ONE NEW YORK PLAZA

ADDRESS	STORIES	COMPLETION	HEIGHT	ARCHITECT
1 Water Street	50	1969	640 feet	Kahn & Jacobs, William Lescaze & Associates

By the early 1960s, virtually the only skyscrapers being built in New York were those notable for their massive volumes. These boxy buildings neither possessed aesthetic proportions nor took notice of the urban context in their designs. Because of the density of skyscraper building in Lower Manhattan, most of these building complexes were initially concentrated in midtown Manhattan. Among the few exceptions of note in the Financial District were the Chase Manhattan Bank Building (page 38) and the Marine Midland Bank Building (page 40). Both skyscrapers were built north of Wall Street and, seen from Upper New York Bay, lay behind existing buildings with their soaring, slender towers. However, after a huge area along South Street was released for development a few years earlier, by around 1970 the waterfront at the extreme southeast of Manhattan would be radically altered. Gigantic complexes of buildings sprang up in this area, sometimes occupying entire blocks, and because of their angular shapes, proved incapable of blending into existing development.

Just north of the Staten Island Ferry terminal, the first of the new large office buildings to be built in 1969 was One New York Plaza. Unfortunately, the architects decided to erect the rectangular complex lengthways to South Street. With a width of 300 feet and a total height of 640 feet, the facade forms a wall-like bulwark that more or less hides the majority of the buildings lying behind it. The view of the towers of Wall Street across the existing arrangement of lower buildings along the waterfront was thereby permanently destroyed. The most striking feature of One New York Plaza is its unusual facade design. Here, the recessed windows look like punched holes, reminiscent of a waffle iron. On the side facing South Street, a 17-story extension was added, increasing the total floor area of the complex to more than 2.4 million square feet.

above: Total view of the building from the north-west
below: General view from the south

55 WATER STREET

ADDRESS	STORIES	COMPLETION	HEIGHT	ARCHITECT
55 WATER STREET	53	1972	687 FEET	EMERY ROTH & SONS

With over 30 million square feet of new floor space to its credit, the architectural firm of Emery Roth & Sons was responsible for approximately one-third of all the office space built in New York between 1950 and 1972. Its architects designed efficient skyscrapers equipped with large offices, advanced air-conditioning systems, and high-speed elevators. Occasionally, these structures altered the character of entire streets. The compact and functional complexes reached a high point in the early 1970s with the commission of 55 Water Street. When this new project was completed, it constituted the largest, private office skyscraper in the world. With a gross floor area of almost 3.5 million square feet, it replaced the Pan Am Building (page 114) as the previous record-holder. Even the almost twice as tall Empire State Building (page 74) could boast of a floor area of "only" 2.3 million square feet.

55 Water Street was part of the large-scale project that envisioned the redesign of the East River waterfront to incorporate large-volume skyscrapers. The 53-story office complex was built on a four-acre block assembled from four contiguous plots. In order to obtain building permits for the project, a portion of the site had to be reserved as public space. Other conditions included the restoration of Jeanette Park on the south side and the construction of a separate subway entrance for the planned East River Line that, however, was never built.

The facades consist of green-tinted glass divided by reinforced concrete supports. In the lower quarter of the buildings these are crossed by decorative horizontal girders. They end on the 15th floor, parallel to the top of the 15-floor extension on the north side, which likewise belongs to the complex and is set back some yards from South Street. At the foot is an elevated plaza, separated from traffic—a condition for obtaining building permits. In the course of a recently undertaken redesign, a 50-foot light, "Beacon of Progress," was installed in the landscaped area, as a tribute to the Titanic Memorial Lighthouse that once stood on the spot.

Only one year after its completion, 55 Water Street lost its title of largest skyscraper in the world (based on gross floor area) to the Twin Towers of the World Trade Center (page 54). Since the violent destruction of the towers, this building is once again the largest office building in New York. With its spacious floors stacked at regular intervals, 55 Water Street remains today a monument to the compact super-buildings of the early 1970s.

above: Looking upwards along the facade of 55 Water Street
below: "Beacon of Progress"

120 WALL STREET

ADDRESS	STORIES	COMPLETION	HEIGHT	ARCHITECT
120 Wall Street	33	1930	399 feet	Ely Jacques Kahn

120 Wall Street with Continental Center (right)

Standing at the eastern end of Wall Street, number 120 stands as a kind of lookout for the skyscrapers that loom behind it in the Financial District. When it was completed in 1930, this 33-story structure was the first major office building to be constructed on the East River waterfront. Although it has meanwhile been surrounded by noticeably larger skyscrapers, its massive flat shape and its facade clad in white brick still create a conspicuous presence on this section of South Street.

The stepped design of 120 Wall Street is based on the requirements established by the New York Zoning Resolution of 1916. Skyscrapers built in accordance with these regulations often have a tower superstructure on top of a base with setbacks. Buildings that dispensed with the tower were unofficially known as "wedding cake" buildings. One such building is 120 Wall Street, which features a 15-story base. With each level containing 25,000 square feet of floor space, these stories account for the overwhelming proportion of the gross floor area of 600,000 square feet. Above this are seven symmetrically arranged setbacks, each embracing two or three stories and giving the upper part of the building the shape of a stepped pyramid.

The bottom five stories of 120 Wall Street are clad in light limestone, with white brick facing above. The profile of the facade is designed so that the emphasis is neither vertical nor horizontal. It also dispenses with the ornamentation frequently used in contemporary buildings. In order to obtain the prestigious Wall Street address, the entrance to the building with its gleaming diagonal steel struts was placed on the narrower south side, which received less daylight.

Entrance on Wall Street

The bottom two stories are notable for their wide windows with polished red-granite frames. The pink marble clad lobby as well as the facade design lack the kind of decorative elements frequently used at the time. In his buildings the architect, Ely Jacques Kahn, placed great importance on not using expensive materials extravagantly. In his view, buildings should attract attention for their design and not because of opulent ornamentation. The skyscrapers he designed were impressive mainly in their detailing rather than by means of eye-catching projections. In the early 1980s, the 554-foot Continental Center was constructed on the adjacent site to the north. Its glazed curtain wall generates an exciting contrast with its neighbor. This impression is reinforced still further by reflection of the stepped stone facade of 120 Wall Street in the dark green glass facade of the modern office building.

AMERICAN INTERNATIONAL BUILDING

(FORMERLY CITIES SERVICE BUILDING; 70 PINE STREET)

ADDRESS	STORIES	COMPLETION	HEIGHT	ARCHITECT
70 Pine Street	67	1932	952 feet (849 feet without mast)	Clinton & Russell

Top of the American International Building

When it was completed in 1932, the Cities Service Building (now American International Building) would be the last major new skyscraper to be constructed in downtown Manhattan for many years. The effects of the Great Depression and the financial constraints during and after World War II meant it would be almost 30 years before another major building could be constructed in the Financial District. With a height of 952 feet this skyscraper surpassed all other buildings in the area and remained the third-tallest building in the world until 1969. Structurally, it is based on a 24,000-ton steel frame.

The intention of the client, the petroleum-refining Cities Service Company (today CITGO), wanted the soaring building to reflect the company's strengths. The resulting skyscraper is one of the best-proportioned high-rises in the city. Above the multiple setbacks of the base rises a noticeably slender tower with multi-profiled angles. The capital of the building with its ornamented, shallow setbacks is one of the most elegant skyscraper terminations ever produced. The uppermost part of the building is clad in a light limestone, conveying the impression of a snow-covered mountaintop. The upper section features a small glass-enclosed observation deck. The story below contains a leather-paneled conference room with an open deck attached to it. Both levels are now reserved for the senior management of the American International Group. In the evening, the capital and its 100-foot mast are illuminated by red, white, and green floodlights. The lobby is notable for its Art Deco features and marble-lined interior in black and pink tones. 10-foot models of the building are carved into the stone of both central pillars at the entrance on Pine Street.

Despite its substantial height, the American International Building has a gross floor area of only 860,000 square feet. It was this aspect that encouraged the commissioning of Otis's first double-decker elevators. The two-story cabins could serve an even and odd story at the same time, which meant less room was needed for the elevator shafts. (Because of its minimal plot size, the building, from an economic point of view, should have had only 48 stories.) Despite this not inconsiderable argument in its favor, the new cabin system failed to gain acceptance in its day. Its rejection by users meant that it was later replaced by conventional elevators. Only 40 years later the construction of double-decker elevators was resumed, since they were especially cost-efficient in extremely tall slender towers. In the mid-1970s the American International insurance group bought the skyscraper on Pine Street and undertook extensive renovations. The work now included an overhaul of the elevator system, the installation of new windows, and the restoration of the facade. A bridge at the 15th story linking the building to a structure opposite on Wall Street had been removed 10 years earlier.

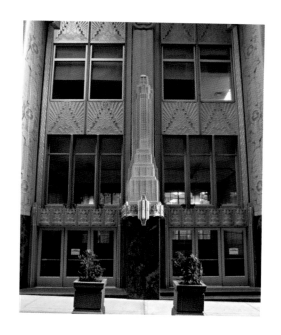

Entrance on Pine Street

60 WALL STREET

(FORMERLY JP MORGAN HEADQUARTERS)

ADDRESS	STORIES	COMPLETION	HEIGHT	ARCHITECT
60 Wall Street	50	1989	745 feet	Kevin Roche, John Dinkeloo & Associates

Since it was built in 1989, the high-rise structure at 60 Wall Street has been one of the largest skyscrapers in the Financial District. In the late 1980s, at the pinnacle of postmodernism, building activity flourished mainly in midtown Manhattan, where there was enough land available for major projects. On Wall Street, where the density of skyscrapers reached a maximum early on, the 50-story building remains the only example from this epoch. Its contextual neoclassical facade also functions as an extension of the surrounding buildings, paying them tribute in its use of mirror glass, which reflects the earlier buildings in all their glory.

The major difference between postmodernist skyscrapers and their counterparts of the 1920s and 1930s is the distinctly larger floor plan of the shaft in the newer buildings. Whereas older high-rises consist of a tiered base on which a slender tower was often constructed, the ambition of the new generation of skyscrapers was not only to be aesthetically pleasing but also to make large amounts of floor space available on the upper floors. With an area of almost 30,000 square feet per floor, 60 Wall Street is able to provide extensive office space on the upper stories whose value is roughly triple that of earlier generations of towers of comparable height (because of zoning ordinances of the day, floor plans of that size were allowed only at the lower levels, which received little daylight). With a gross floor area of 1.7 million square feet, the American headquarters of Deutsche Bank is accordingly larger than every other building on Wall Street. In order to obtain a building permit in an area with notoriously strict regulations, the air rights of 55 Wall Street, which stands opposite, had to be bought up and transferred to the new building project.

The design by the architectural firm Kevin Roche, John Dinkeloo & Associates, features a mixture of creativity and functionality. The tower with profiled edges stands on a flat platform. Its horizontally accentuated facade has a blue-tinted mirror-glass cladding, with bands of light-gray granite at the edges. The capital comprises the top seven stories, and is flanked at the corners by pairs of faceted columns. In conjunction with the sliced pyramidal roof, the upper quarter of the buildings takes on the form of a classical temple placed on the shaft. At street level a spacious arcade runs from Wall Street to Pine Street, and is notable for its golden mosaic ceiling with recessed lattices and octagonal columns. There is seating in the form of granite benches beside small café tables, surrounded by sculptures and palms. In the spring of 2007 the Paramount Group bought the 745-foot complex from Deutsche Bank for $1.2 billion—the highest amount ever paid for an office building in downtown Manhattan.

above: View from the east side
below: Arcade between Wall Street and Pine Street

CHASE MANHATTAN BANK BUILDING

(ALSO KNOWN AS ONE CHASE MANHATTAN PLAZA)

ADDRESS	STORIES	COMPLETION	HEIGHT	ARCHITECT
1 CHASE MANHATTAN PLAZA	60	1961	813 FEET	GORDON BUNSHAFT OF SKIDMORE, OWINGS & MERRILL

Chase Manhattan Bank was born of the merger of the Bank of Manhattan with Chase National Bank in 1955. The management of the newly formed company decided shortly thereafter to build a new headquarters north of Wall Street. Aiming to counter the migration of banks toward midtown Manhattan, which had been the trend since the 1950s, this was a deliberate decision, even though the area around the New York Stock Exchange was considerably more expensive than land farther north. When the Chase Manhattan Bank Building opened its doors in 1961 after almost four years of construction, it was the first new skyscraper building in downtown Manhattan of note in almost 30 years. This monumental steel-frame structure also introduced the International Style to the Financial District, creating a marked contrast with the skyscrapers built during previous periods.

above: Total view from the south side
below: The sculpture *Group of Four Trees*

To comply with New York building regulations, the project included two complete blocks covering a total area of two and a half acres. The cost of the land for the downtown location alone ran to what was then a record price of $100 million. The construction costs for the 60-story tower, which occupies less than 30 percent of the site, amounted to an additional $121 million. With the revision of building regulations in the early 1960s, public plazas had already become a familiar sight in midtown Manhattan. The plaza in front of the Chase Manhattan Bank Building, completed in 1962, was the first in the Financial District. One Chase Manhattan Plaza stands on a raised platform, and is linked with street traffic via a ramp. 10 years later, a 43-foot sculpture called *Group of Four Trees* by the French artist Jean Dubuffet was installed in the plaza. Weighing 25 tons, the sculpture is positioned east of the Isamu Noguchi-designed Sunken Garden completed eight years earlier. Located 16 feet below the plaza, the Noguchi garden is embellished with a fountain and basalt stones. On the north side, the plaza leads directly into the spacious entrance lobby. Along with 48 elevators, the lobby also features art from the bank's collections. With the exception of the top story, only the lower floors are used by what is now JP Morgan Chase. The largest percentage of the 1.9 million square feet gross floor area is used by other tenant companies.

With a height of 813 feet, the Chase Manhattan Bank Building is still one of the highest structures in the Financial District. Its facade consists of a glazed curtain wall notable for the facings between the floors and continuous vertical mullions. The anodized aluminum-clad supports are found exclusively on the 290-foot-wide north and south sides. Together with the core of the building, they form the load-bearing elements of the complex. The load-bearing system used in this case permitted greater flexibility in the design of the floor plans. At the time the structure was built, however, it was not possible to dispense entirely with supporting pillars in the interior. An additional problem for the stability of the structure was the absence of cross struts. In contrast to the tubular system later used, these support elements had not yet been developed at the time of completion. To solve the problem, architect Gordon Bunshaft had the horizontal girders made at twice their usual thickness.

MARINE MIDLAND BANK BUILDING

(ALSO KNOWN AS HSBC BANK BUILDING)

ADDRESS	STORIES	COMPLETION	HEIGHT	ARCHITECT
140 BROADWAY	52	1967	688 FEET	GORDON BUNSHAFT OF SKIDMORE, OWINGS & MERRILL

The Marine Midland Bank Building represents Gordon Bunshaft's development of his design for the Chase Manhattan Bank Building, constructed six years earlier (page 38). As a result of a bend in Liberty Street, the Marine Midland Bank Building has a trapezoidal floor plan. The tapering of the site toward Broadway had a direct influence on the design of the building in that the four structural bays on the east side are reduced to three on the west. In terms of adapting to an existing street pattern, the building is one of the few sucessful examples from the 1960s of responsible urban development in New York.

The decision to use a surface of dark tinted glass was a direct result of the influence of the CBS Building on the Avenue of the Americas (page 154), completed two years earlier. The window units of the Marine Midland Bank Building are separated by matte, bronze-colored aluminum spandrels. Similar to the Chase Manhattan Bank Building, the facings were coated with corrosion-proofing material. In combination with the thin mullions, the facade acquired a smooth grid design. With its homogeneous surface, the 52-story tower was one of the last of its kind to represent the standardized modernist style. With the International Style thus fully mined, where to go next was something that only postmodernism could answer in the 1980s.

From its south side, Marine Midland Bank Building is only a short distance from the Equitable Building (page 18). As a result, this segment of Cedar Street presents an extremely narrow corridor that degenerates into a gloomy urban canyon. The unfortunate urban-planning and economic effects of overly dense development were intended to have been prevented by the first zoning ordinance, the New York Zoning Resolution of 1916. Following the revision of the ordinance in the early 1960s, dark corridors of this kind became possible once again.

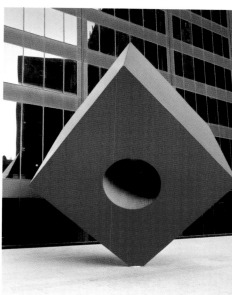

above: Total view from the west side
below: *Red Cube* by Isamu Noguchi

The plaza on the west side, however, expresses the positive aspects of the changes in the law. As a result of the tower being set back 100 feet from the sidewalks of Broadway, the densely developed street is interrupted. In the plaza, at the northwest edge of the building stands Isamu Noguchi's 26-foot high sculpture *Red Cube*—a red-painted steel cubic form balanced on one corner, with a large cylindrical hole in the center.

CIVIC CENTER TO BATTERY PARK CITY

Skyscraper development along lower Broadway includes a number of contrasting architectural styles. Along Park Row are some of the oldest skyscrapers in New York, whereas Battery Park City, at the extreme southwestern tip of Manhattan, features new office and apartment buildings. While less densely developed than the Financial District, the area contains iconic buildings in various styles within a relatively small area, ranging from the neoclassical Woolworth Building to the Barclay-Vesey Building (the first Art Deco skyscraper) to the complex of postmodernist office buildings of the World Financial Center. The World Financial Center buildings were erected on landfill comprised of excavations taken during the construction of the World Trade Center. The Trade Center's Twin Towers dominated the skyline of downtown Manhattan for almost 30 years until they were violently destroyed on September 11, 2001. Their former location—now called Ground Zero—is the largest construction site in New York.

KEY

14 **Park Row Building**

15 **Municipal Building**

16 **Woolworth Building**

17 **Barclay-Vesey Building**

18 **World Trade Center**

19 **World Financial Center**

20 **One Liberty Plaza**

2

PARK ROW BUILDING

ADDRESS	STORIES	COMPLETION	HEIGHT	ARCHITECT
15 PARK ROW	30	1899	391 FEET	ROBERT H. ROBERTSON

At the end of the 19th century, a series of office towers built succes-sively on Park Row vied for the title of tallest building in the world. The buildings primarily housed the offices of the major U.S. dailies, and this section of the street was also known as "Newspaper Row". The St. Paul Building supplanted the World Building as the tall-est on Park Row in 1898, and one year later the Park Row Building brought an impressive end to the rivalry. With a height of 391 feet, it held the title of the world's tallest building until the completion of the Singer Building in 1908. Its 30 stories were also a record for their day.

A typical feature of the structures of the time was limiting the confinement of ornamentation to the main facades. The facades on the side streets or the rear of the building were generally neglected in terms of embellishment and very plain in design. In the case of the Park Row Building, the opulently decorated main facade of the cornice courses is divided into six horizontal units, which tends to minimize the impression of height rather than reinforce it. The up-per termination of the building is formed by turret structures with copper-clad cupolas. In the original plans, these were intended to house a pair of observatories. Although the two features lend the Park Row Building a distinctive character, they also reduce its scale. In general, the terminations of New York skyscrapers around the turn of the century suffered from the problem of being neither original nor unified. This historical confusion was not really solved until the arrival of the homogeneously designed setback skyscrap-ers of the 1920s.

From the 105-foot-wide main facade of the Park Row Building, the north and south sides extend to describe a trapezoidal ground plan, with a narrower facade at the east end. The surfaces of the three facades consist of unmodulated brick masonry. On Ann Street two interior courtyards allow daylight into the inner offices. The core of the marble-lined lobby is formed by 10 elevators ar-ranged in a semicircular bay. In the building's 1,000 offices, almost 4,000 employees are at work during peak times. With its extensive square footage, the building (long the headquarters of Associated Press) was a forerunner of the office complexes that would be built in the years to come.

In June 1999, the New York City Landmarks Preservation Com-mission designated as a landmark the Park Row Building, one of the last surviving 19th-century skyscrapers. Two years later, sub-stantial renovation work was undertaken at a cost of $30 million, during which time the floors above the 11th story were converted into 210 residential units.

above: Tower structures over the main facade
below: Facade decoration of the Park Row Building

MUNICIPAL BUILDING

ADDRESS	STORIES	COMPLETION	HEIGHT	ARCHITECT
1 Centre Street	34	1914	580 feet	William M. Kendall of McKim, Mead & White

Greater New York was created by the consolidation of Manhattan with Brooklyn, Queens, Staten Island, and the Bronx in 1898. A short time later, city administrators decided to establish a new joint seat of government for the new combined borough. After a competitive bid, the submission by the reputable firm of McKim, Mead & White was awarded the contract for implementing the new project. The firm's Municipal Building design represents a successful attempt to combine Beaux-Arts classicism with the skyscraper configuration. One of the basic stipulations behind this project was the emphasis on relating it to the urban fabric. The city should "pass through" the Municipal Building and not, as had been the case with many of its predecessors, detour around it. The arched structure over Chambers Street therefore was not the innovative suggestion of architect William M. Kendall but a requirement of the client. The client also specified that the building be connected to the subway system. With its entrance to the subway incorporated into the ground floor, the Municipal Building became the prototype skyscraper with a direct link to public transportation.

The large scale of the Municipal Building made up for its lack of real innovation by the successful use of classical elements. It featured a tripartite division, beginning with an open, three-story pedestal surrounded by Corinthian columns. Still today, this serves as a stylistic echo of the monumental municipal and judicial buildings in the immediate vicinity. The base segues into a 24-story shallow U-shaped shaft clad with light-gray Maine granite. The massive center section terminates in a colonnade on the top four floors, which forms a pendant to the colonnade at street level. The opulently decorated capital above consists of a tapering tower structure that is also surrounded by columns. This topmost unit alone makes up one-third of the total building height and is surrounded at its podium by four smaller pointed turrets. These are intended to symbolize the four boroughs merged with Manhattan. At the top is Adolph A. Weinman's statue *Civic Fame*. 20 feet high, it is the largest statue in New York (the much larger Statue of Liberty is actually under the shared jurisdiction of New York and New Jersey).

The horizontal emphasis of the Municipal Building conflicts with a striving for prominent height. From a distance, the building looks more like a solid wall than a skyscraper. In the ensuing years, its design proved

above: View from the south
below: The icon bearing capital of the Municipal Building

inspirational for numerous architects. Well-known examples of similar designs are the Wrigley Building in Chicago, the Cleveland Terminal Tower, and Moscow State University. With a gross floor area of approximately 850,000 square feet, the Municipal Building was when it opened one of the largest buildings in New York. The long construction period of five years exceeded the norm and attested to the enormous effort demanded from the institutions involved in this project. The New York City Landmarks Preservation Commission duly honored its unusual position in municipal history in 1966, when the building became one of the first to be designated a historic landmark.

WOOLWORTH BUILDING

ADDRESS	STORIES	COMPLETION	HEIGHT	ARCHITECT
233 Broadway	57	1913	792 FEET	Cass Gilbert

When on April 24, 1913, President Woodrow Wilson flipped the switch turning on the 80,000 light bulbs of the Woolworth Building from the White House in Washington, D.C., he marked the opening of one of the most important monuments in the history of skyscrapers. The client for the "cathedral of commerce," which held the title of tallest building in the world for the next 17 years, was Frank Winfield Woolworth. Owner of the Woolworth "five-and-dime" chain of stores, he was one of the richest Americans of his day. The aim of the new company headquarters was to offset the down-market image of his low-cost variety stores. Woolworth paid the $13.5 million for the new building in cash.

Beginning with the foundation, the building's structural engineers faced a hitherto unparalleled challenge. With the load-bearing foundation stone set 100 feet below ground, the structure had to be supported by concrete pillars reaching down to bedrock level, to prevent any major shift in the building's center of gravity. Complete with flying buttresses, pointed turrets, and waterspouts, the exterior has a late-Gothic look. These features were particularly appropriate for the vertical emphasis that Louis Sullivan sought in his building designs. Massing is distributed in such a way that the building can be viewed as a tower or an urban office block. The 27-story base is U-shaped, opening toward the west facade, which is oriented away from Broadway.

Above the center of the east facade is a 30-story tower. This unit is not set back from the base but instead forms a natural extension of the base. This illusion of continuity is reinforced by the vertical lines of the supporting pillars and window mullions, which are embellished with terra-cotta ornamentation. The tower terminates in an ornate crown decorated with pinnacles and surmounted by a copper-clad pyramidal roof and lantern. At night, the building is floodlit and the upper elements appear bathed in white light.

The modern mechanical installations inside the steel-frame building contrast with the exterior features, which are more in keeping with the late Middle Ages. Along with its own generator, which can produce enough power to illuminate a city of 50,000 people, the building has AC-operated high-speed elevators. With a vertical speed of more than 650 feet per minute, these were the most modern and fastest elevators of their day. Two of the 29 in total are express elevators zooming directly to the 54th floor. Unfortunately, the observation deck above that level has been off-limits to the public since 1945.

above: Aerial view
center: Top of the Woolworth Building
below: Entrance on Broadway

above: Elaborate ceiling mosaic by Charles A. Platt
left: Entrance hall in the west wing

The two-story Romanesque-style lobby resembles a giant ornamental casket. Notable among the many high-quality art works in the entrance lobby are Charles A. Platt's ceiling mosaics, which allow visitors to easily forget that they are inside a 20th-century skyscraper. On the galleries above the north and south entrances are the murals *Labor* and *Commerce*, which symbolize Woolworth's ideals of work and trade. As in the great medieval cathedrals, the patrons, architects, and artisans associated with the building's creation are immortalized in sculptures. Among these figures is the architect Cass Gilbert cradling a model of the building, the structural engineer Gunvald Aus measuring a steel beam, and Frank Woolworth counting coins. Among other carved ornaments of wood and marble, the elevator doors are lavishly adorned with various bronze motifs.

Within a gross floor area of about 1.0 million square feet, up to 14,000 people were employed during the building's early years. At that time, Woolworth's headquarters occupied only a small fraction of the floors. Other tenants included the Irving Trust Company Bank and Columbia Records, which had a recording studio in the building. After the Woolworth chain went out of business in the late 1990s, the building, which up to that time had never been encumbered with mortgage, changed hands for the first time in 1998 when it was sold to a developer for $155 million. Initial plans to convert the top 25 stories into condominium units were in the meantime scuttled. After extensive renovation work, the lavishly appointed office floors in the tower area featured (among other amenities) direct access to the observation deck on the 55th floor.

Few buildings in the world have acquired as many popular nicknames as the Woolworth Building. Shortly it opened, it was dubbed a "cathedral of commerce," "office basilica," and "five and dime cathedral." In more recent times it has been called the "Mozart of skyscrapers." Even after nearly a century, this masterpiece of Beaux-Arts classicism is still one of the best-known skyscrapers in the world. At the beginning of the 20th century, its high-speed elevators and nighttime floodlighting established a new stylistic precedent. The symbolism it exudes, based on a perfect harmony of cutting-edge technology and well-proportioned massing, would be of pioneering importance for future generations of skyscrapers. On the occasion of its 70th anniversary, in April 1983, the building's architectural features were given official landmark status by the New York City Landmarks Preservation Commission. Seventeen years earlier, the U.S. Department of the Interior had accorded it the status of a National Historic Landmark.

Caricatures of Frank W. Woolworth (top) and Cass Gilbert (below) in the arcades

BARCLAY-VESEY BUILDING

(ALSO KNOWN AS NEW YORK TELEPHONE COMPANY BUILDING; VERIZON BUILDING)

ADDRESS	STORIES	COMPLETION	HEIGHT	ARCHITECT
140 WEST STREET	32	1927	498 FEET	RALPH WALKER OF MCKENZIE, VOORHEES & GMELIN

Built for the New York Telephone Company, the Barclay-Vesey Building acquired architectural prominence with an exterior profile that appeared to effortlessly bridge the chasm between classicism and modernism. At the date of its completion, the building had no definable relationship with any historical style. What are today the familiar Art Deco skyscrapers were either still under construction or on the drawing board, so the building, which won several architectural awards, also can be considered the first Art Deco skyscraper.

The steel-frame structure clad with brown brick was based on the latest technological advancements, reinforced by a central core. Its parallelogram-shaped ground plan occupies a 52,000 square-foot site between Barclay and Vesey Street. As the interior of the building's base was dedicated to telephone equipment, the architect dispensed with unnecessary light wells. The middle area of the building contains several unobtrusive setbacks, and has an H-shaped ground plan. At the 18th-floor level, a massive tower springs from the center of the building, slightly rotated in relation to the main structure, giving the viewer regarding the building in its entirety the impression of an oblique angle.

The driving force of this new building project lay in considering the design in the context of cost-effectiveness. Although under existing building regulations, the tower could have been built considerably higher, the building's height of 498 feet was arrived at by a strict calculation of projected costs and revenues. Architect Ralph Walker opted for a fundamentally plain design for the structure, but he did not completely eliminate ornamentation. To accentuate the rise of the capital, elephant and ram's heads as well as bird and pineapple motifs of light-colored limestone—reflecting the Art Deco predilection for organic elements—were worked into edges and terminations.

When the facades of the Barclay-Vesey Building were heavily damaged by falling masonry from the World Trade Center (page 54) following the terrorist attacks on September 11, 2001, these decorative motifs were particularly hard hit. It took two years of restoration work to repair the damage.

In the lobby, which extends from Washington Street to West Street, are bronze engravings depicting scenes from the construction of New York's telephone network system, and a sumptuous ceiling painting illustrates the history of communications. At the beginning of the 20th century, the block on which the Barclay-Vesey Building now stands was adjacent to the Hudson River piers. After the building was completed, an attempt was made to erect an attractive row of shops around the arcades on Vesey Street, but with the location being away from the busy shopping streets, the idea proved impracticable. When a connection to its infrastructure was finally established with the construction of the World Trade Center in the early 1970s, retail stores moved into the World Trade Center's underground shopping malls.

above: View from the west
below: Entrance on West Street

WORLD TRADE CENTER

ADDRESS	STORIES	COMPLETION	HEIGHT	ARCHITECT
World Trade Center	110 each	1973; destroyed: 2001	One World Trade Center: 1,368 feet (1,728 feet incl. radio mast) Two World Trade Center: 1,362 feet	Minoru Yamasaki, Emery Roth & Sons

On the morning of September 11, 2001, two passenger airliners hijacked by terrorists were deliberately crashed into Buildings One (or the North Tower) and Two (or the South Tower) of the World Trade Center. As the gasoline on the planes caught fire, several building floors burst into flame within a few minutes. When the steel joist suspensions buckled as the heat soared to more than 1500°F, they were no longer able to bear the weight of the floors, and gave way. About an hour after the collisions, the domino effect triggered by the falling floors caused the towers to collapse completely within a few seconds. Among the more than 2,800 victims were not only the passengers of the airplanes and people working on the upper floors of the towers but also 300 firefighters and police officers. Because of the heroism of emergency service workers and many civilian volunteers, more than 20,000 people were evacuated from the World Trade Center that morning and survived the catastrophe.

This was not the first terrorist attack on the World Trade Center. On February 26, 1993, six people were killed when a massive car bomb was detonated in the underground parking area. Although considerable damage was caused to the foundations, the external load-bearing system presented no immediate danger of collapse. The second, devastating terrorist attack on 9/11 dramatically altered the skyline of downtown Manhattan—in a reverse of the effect the Twin Towers had produced when they were erected in the early 1970s, after six years of construction.

The total costs of this gigantic construction project ran to more than $1 billion. In total, more than 180,000 tons of steel and 12 million cubic feet of concrete were used. To build the foundations, almost 35 million cubic feet of mica schist had to be excavated, which was used to create the landfill along the Hudson River that would eventually become the site of Battery Park City. The Twin Towers were aligned diagonally from each other only 44 yards apart, with square ground plans measuring 208 feet per side. They soared to a height of 1,368 and 1,362 feet, respectively, without interruption or setbacks, snatching away from the Empire State Building (page 74) the title of tallest building in the world after more than 40 years. The gross floor area of more than 4.6 million square feet for each tower also set a new record that remained until the buildings' destruction. Apart from the

above: Terrorist attack from September 11, 2001
right: Rendering for the rebuilding of the World Trade Center site

Twin Towers, the complex also included three low buildings, a hotel, and the 47-story Seven World Trade Center on Vesey Street. With the exception of Seven World Trade Center, these structures stood on a fifteen-acre plaza, in the middle of which was a fountain and bronze sculpture by the German artist Fritz König. The globe-like sculpture was rescued from the ruins after the attacks of 9/11, and was placed in its badly damaged state in nearby Battery Park as a memorial.

Architect Minoru Yamasaki attempted to compensate for the rather banal appearance of the towers by designing them as a pair and aligning them on a diagonal, as noted. In the view of many critics, however, their uniformity and boxy shape are essentially unimaginative, their huge masses making the more lively buildings in the vicinity seem smaller than they really were. From an aesthetic point of view, with their location west of the Financial District, the towers made Lower Manhattan, which up to then had presented a uniform, organic silhouette, look unfinished.

above: Aerial view of Ground Zero
below: *The Sphere Memorial* in Battery Park

The facades of the Twin Towers consisted of lattices of vertical steel supports. Since the supports were only two feet apart, glass represented only 30 percent of the surface area. Together with the transverse struts, the aluminum-clad columns formed a rigid tube that carried the horizontal and vertical loads of the building. The floor plates, which were only three inches thick, were tied to the external frame and supported on concrete-trussed steel suspensions. With this lightweight structural system, only half the amount of steel was needed, in comparison with earlier generations of skyscrapers. In addition, with the relaxing of building and fire codes in 1968, fewer stairwells were required than previously. Revised again in the 1980s, these regulations allowed for a more cost-efficient use of floor space. In hindsight, however, they can be considered partly responsible for the relatively rapid collapse of the towers of the World Trade Center and for virtually preventing any possibility of escape above the point of impact.

Many technical innovations were first used in the World Trade Center. Along with an automatic washing system for the 43,600 windows in each tower, a new elevator system was also developed for the buildings. Because of the large numbers of floors, and to prevent unnecessary space being wasted on elevator shafts in the lower floors, the vertical transport of people

The new Seven World Trade Center

was carried out primarily by 23 express elevators. These ferried workers at different intervals up to the "sky lobbies" on the 44th and 78th floors. From these levels, local elevators stopped at individual floors. In the World Trade Center complex as a whole, more than 50,000 people were employed and worked in a gross floor area of 12 million square feet. The building was designed so that people could reach their workplaces directly from their homes via the subway station integrated into the basement. In addition to employees, up to 80,000 visitors a day entered the complex. Many of them visited the observation deck in the South Tower or the Windows of the World restaurant on the 107th floor of the North Tower, which had a spectacular view.

It took nearly six months to clear the debris from the ruins of the World Trade Center at Ground Zero and the surrounding area. In February 2003, architect Daniel Libeskind won the competition for the redesign of the site. His master plan envisioned a complex of five angular skyscrapers grouped around a park-like landscape. The former foundations of the World Trade Center were to include a memorial to the victims of 9/11. The plans were altered several times under the influence of Larry Silverstein, the site's developer, who exerted his influence and brought in David Childs as executive architect in the summer of 2003. The tallest of the office towers, Freedom Tower, according to the most recent designs, is intended to stand on a 200-foot-high base, with a shaft of 82 stories and an observation deck rising from it. At a height of 1,776 feet with its superstructure, Freedom Tower will be the tallest building in the city upon its projected completion in 2011. In 2006, published plans for the other towers on the site envisioned three differently structured office buildings ranging from 975 to 1,350 feet high. The first of the destroyed buildings to be rebuilt was Seven World Trade Center, which reopened in the summer of 2006. In contrast with the polished granite cladding of its predecessor, the 741-foot-high office complex is clad with a curtain wall of blue tinted glass. Responding to the tragedy of 9/11, the Childs design conforms to the highest safety standards with respect to stability requirements and evacuation routes.

WORLD FINANCIAL CENTER

ADDRESS	STORIES	COMPLETION	HEIGHT	ARCHITECT
Liberty Street and Vesey Street, between West Street and Hudson River	34–51	1985–87	500–739 feet	Cesar Pelli & Associates

The World Financial Center, built in the mid-1980s, stands as New York's largest project for a unified urban complex since the construction of Rockefeller Center (page 150). As had been the case some 50 years earlier, contextualizing the buildings was a key challenge. With their tiered masonry facades and varied terminations, the four postmodernist office towers create a visual axis extending to the existing landscape. Even though glass makes up a larger proportion of the surfaces than in the case of the older structures, it was nonetheless the most successful construction project in the 1980s to preserve the New York skyscraper tradition.

In the late 1970s the landfill created by the dumping of excavated material from the World Trade Center (page 54) was released as developable land. The contract for the design of the $1.2-billion project was awarded to architect Cesar Pelli. His design called for four skyscrapers on a square ground plan. Because of their large sites, the buildings, which vary in height from 500 to 739 feet, have a total floor area of 8.5 million square feet. Their differing heights and positions were prescribed by the city, which wanted them to relate to adjacent developments. Thus the roof of One World Financial Center forms a counterpart to the West Street Building opposite, while the tower of Three World Financial Center is rotated on its base like the neighboring Barclay-Vesey Building (page 52).

Aerial view of the buildings in their urban context

below: View from the Hudson River

The facades of the office towers are clad with polished granite and reflective glass. The distribution of these two different materials is intended to create a kind of time capsule of the development of New York skyscrapers over the past 60 years. The granite-clad base has modest setbacks reminiscent of prewar skyscrapers. With every setback, more glass appears in the surface, and the proportion of granite cladding decreases accordingly. The upper stories with their glazed curtain wall represent classic modernism. The four differently shaped roof profiles symbolize the transition from modernism to the more abstract postmodernist period. The different reflective characteristics of the facade surfaces stand out particularly at sunset: artificial light is by then visible through the windows of the base floors, while the glass curtain wall of the upper levels still reflects the last rays of sun in the evening sky. The construction of the World Financial Center was of critical importance for Lower Manhattan's skyline in another respect as well. After the completion of the World Trade Center 15 years earlier, the skyline had begun to acquire a lopsided appearance. The buildings now constructed west of the Twin Towers managed to reinstate a more rounded, harmonious termination.

The main attraction for visitors to the World Financial Center is its winter garden built in 1988, between Two and Three World Financial Center. Its glass cupola carried on a steel skeleton is 125 feet high and 200 feet long on an east-west axis. Cafés, several small shops, and palm trees from the Mojave Desert are distributed over a ground area of 18,000 square feet. A wide set of marble steps forms the centerpiece of the Winter Garden. Apart from various exhibitions and performances, concerts are regularly held here as well.

Like all the other parts of the World Financial Center, the Winter Garden was damaged during the terrorist attack of 9/11. Falling debris from the Twin Towers destroyed large parts of its glass roof and steel frame. After a $50 million renovation, it was ceremonially reopened exactly a year later. The southeast facade of Three World Financial Center suffered similar damage. In contrast to the other three buildings, several supporting elements were also destroyed. Even so, all employees were back in their workplaces within six months.

The World Financial Center constitutes only a part of the total development on new sites in southwest Manhattan. The Battery Park City area between West Street and the Hudson River saw the construction not only of new office buildings but also several apartment complexes. A condition for granting building permission was that public space be provided at the same time. Plantings and small parks, a number of sports facilities, and a nicely laid-out promenade banked along the Hudson River now account for almost half the nearly 100-acre site.

above: Office towers of the World Financial Center at sunset
below: Winter garden of the World Financial Center
left: Western entrance of the winter garden

ONE LIBERTY PLAZA

(FORMERLY U.S. STEEL BUILDING)

above: *Double Check* in Zuccotti Park
below: Singer Building (1908–1968)

ADDRESS	STORIES	COMPLETION	HEIGHT	ARCHITECT
165 Broadway	54	1973	743 feet	Roy Allen of Skidmore, Owings & Merrill

In the same way that the Equitable Building (page 18), located diagonally opposite, symbolizes the end of the period of unregulated construction at the beginning of the 20th century, so One Liberty Plaza bears witness to the end of the stripping down to essentials that Mies van der Rohe advocated. The two buildings have another feature in common as well. Both consist of stacks of evenly spaced stories intended to ideally utilize the volume of the building. The facade of One Liberty Plaza, with its display of steel girders piled one on top of the other, reflects the business of its developer, the U.S. Steel Corporation. Together with the Chase Manhattan Bank Building (page 38) and the Marine Midland Bank Building (page 40), it forms part of an east-west axis of immense skyscrapers surrounded by large plazas.

In contrast to the glazed surfaces of earlier skyscrapers, in One Liberty Plaza it is the steel framework that is given visual emphasis. The structure is held together by massive six-foot steel girders which feature a fire-proof coating. They replace the usual parapets between floors, and together with the core shaft make up the load-bearing elements of the building. As a result, all 54 floors have an unobstructed floor area of 36,000 square feet. Behind the steel joists, the rows of windows mutate into narrow glass slits, prompting a number of architectural critics to complain that this was no longer a glass skyscraper with a steel frame but a steel building with concealed glass apertures.

Until 1968, the 612-foot-high Singer Building, an elegant, slender skyscraper built in a Beaux-Arts style, occupied the site. At its completion in 1908 it was the tallest building in the world, a title it would retain for one year. Economic constraints and the crude treatment of older developments in the 1960s were responsible for the Singer Building having to give way to an office tower with five times as much floor space. (Until the violent destruction of the World Trade Center [page 54], it held the dubious distinction of being the tallest skyscraper ever demolished.) After air rights were transferred to the new building project, a small park feature called Liberty Plaza Park was created on the unbuilt area on the southern edge of the site.

Renamed Zuccotti Park, the plaza was redesigned in the summer of 2006. As well as having trees and benches, it is now adorned with Mark di Suvero's 65-foot steel sculpture *Joie de Vivre*. John Seward Johnson Jr.'s bronze sculpture *Double Check* was also returned to its original location at the northwest corner of the park. When the World Trade Center collapsed on September 11, 2001, the Johnson sculpture, which shows an office worker looking through his briefcase, was covered by debris and dust, making it a kind of interim memorial for the victims of the terrorist attack. This statue was removed after 9/11, having been at that location for 20 years, and then returned when the park renovations were complete in 2006. Like all other skyscrapers in the vicinity, One Liberty Plaza was also damaged by falling debris. Because of its solid structure however, the damage was limited, and the building resumed regular operations after a relatively short time.

CHAPTER

MIDTOWN SOUTH

Most skyscrapers in Midtown South were built during the first half of the 20th century. In 1902 the inauguration of the Flatiron Building, the first skyscraper north of the Civic Center, set the ball in motion. Seven years later the Metropolitan Life Tower, just a few steps to the northeast, was erected, becoming the tallest building in the world at the time. Little by little this district, which extends from 23rd Street as far north as 42nd Street, was built up more and more densely. Its truly outstanding architectural feature—in every sense of the word—is the Empire State Building. No other skyscraper symbolizes high-rise architecture to such a degree or is as widely known as the building that today is still New York's tallest. The American Radiator Building, overlooking Bryant Park, and the Chanin Building, which was constructed during the building boom of the late 1920s, also contributed to the development of the skyscraper.

3

KEY

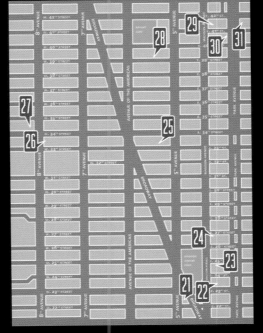

21   Flatiron Building

22   Metropolitan Life Tower

23   Metropolitan Life North Building

24   New York Life Building

25   Empire State Building

26   One Penn Plaza

27   New Yorker Hotel

28   American Radiator Building

29   Lincoln Building

30   100 Park Avenue

31   Chanin Building

FLATIRON BUILDING

(FORMERLY ALSO KNOWN AS THE FULLER BUILDING)

ADDRESS	STORIES	COMPLETION	HEIGHT	ARCHITECT
175 Fifth Avenue	21	1902	285 feet	Daniel H. Burnham & Company

Although the Flatiron Building is by no means New York's first skyscraper, as is sometimes claimed, it holds an extremely significant place in the architectural history of the city. Apart from the public sensation that its completion aroused far beyond the boundaries of New York, it demonstrated for the first time the expansion of high-rise construction into the areas of Manhattan lying north of the Financial District and lower Broadway. The original name, the "Fuller Building," was quickly to be forgotten. Its distinct triangular shape, a result of the fact that the site narrowed to a point as it extended north toward the intersection of Broadway and Fifth Avenue, soon earned it the nickname the "Flatiron Building" among the general public, and today this is its official name. The unusual ground plan of the building makes for a lack of standardized office spaces, but at the same time almost every office unit admits daylight. The Fuller Construction Company, which commissioned the building, also benefited from the illusion it gave of a freestanding structure and its high-profile location.

The tripartite composition of the Flatiron Building corresponds to the model of the classical Greek column, here expanded to form a wall. Broad window frontages and rusticated limestone cladding characterize the lower stories. The shaft directly above has a tapestry-like facade. Its eight-story, slightly curved projecting bays on the sides reveal strong similarities with the skyscrapers of that period in Chicago. Two-story round-headed windows and a wealth of ornamentation are featured at the capital, above which a cornice band, also elaborately decorated, completes the elevation. In order to withstand the pressure of high winds resulting from the location, the steel framework, which is completely covered by the facade cladding, was given especially robust bracing. In the first years after completion strong gusts of wind arose at the rounded end of the building, which is only 6 feet in width. (Given the fashion for long skirts at the time, this provided some entertainment before police put a stop to the pastime.)

Daniel H. Burnham's design for the Flatiron Building represented a retreat from the innovative architecture associated with the architect and his works in Chicago.

above: Elaborate facade decoration at the building's apex
below: View from Madison Square Park

The Beaux-Arts style lent the appearance of bygone ages to these new monumental buildings. Like so many skyscrapers that were constructed subsequently in New York, the Flatiron Building displayed an elaborate mix of Gothic and Renaissance motifs, which were rejected by advocates of the Chicago School.

More than 100 years after its completion, the Flatiron Building is still one of the emblems of New York. As a result of its conspicuous shape and its important role in the further evolution of the skyscraper, in 1966 it was the first building in the city to be granted landmark status by the City of New York. 13 years later it was included in the National Register of Historic Places. For fans of the Spiderman movies it is also famous as the editorial offices of the *Daily Bugle*.

METROPOLITAN LIFE TOWER

ADDRESS	STORIES	COMPLETION	HEIGHT	ARCHITECT
1 MADISON AVENUE	50	1909	700 FEET	NAPOLEON LEBRUN & SONS

In the early 20th century the high-rise architecture of New York relied mainly on historical stylistic elements. The Metropolitan Life Tower represents the pinnacle of this tendency to imitate European buildings. Its great similarity to the Campanile in Venice is undeniable, despite the architect's protestations to the contrary. Pierre LeBrun later spoke of an unconscious absorption that almost inevitably resulted from the requirements of a tall tower with historical detail. In the process the dimensions of this skyscraper were increased to more than twice the size of the original. With a height of 700 feet, the Metropolitan Life Tower surpassed the Singer Building, which had been constructed the previous year, and remained the tallest building in the world for four years.

The tower, which is elongated like a telescope, was completed after a two-year construction period. It is sited on the north side of the insurance headquarters building that had already been constructed in 1893. Because individual elements of the tower were designed to be oversized, it does not appear to be as tall as it really is. The clock faces on the upper part of the shaft extend over three floors. Each of the numbers on the clocks is four feet long and weighs half a ton. The transitional zone from the shaft to the capital, which accounts for one third of the building's total height on its own, is composed of 40-foot-high arcades. Above this the tower is set back and crowned with a pyramidal roof section and finally the bell tower, in which hang four bronze bells weighing between 1,500 pounds and 3.5 tons. The top of the building has a cupola decorated with gold leaf, within which a beacon was installed. Its light, once described in the advertising brochures of the insurance company as "the light that never fails," is to this day a distinctive feature of the New York skyline. Since 1980 the lower part of the capital, too, has been illuminated after dark. The colors can be varied by adding disks in different shades to the floodlights.

The enhanced image that resulted from a skyscraper of these dimensions was important to the company from an early stage. By holding the accolade of the world's tallest building, the Metropolitan Life Insurance Company wished to convey a feeling of stability and success to its customers. In this context it was of secondary importance that the small floor plan of the 50-story tower made its operation unprofitable. The elevator shafts, whose cars were the fastest at that time, with a speed of 590 feet per minute, take up a comparatively large proportion of the floor space of each story.

In the mid-1960s the original marble cladding was replaced by slabs of limestone as part of a major renovation. With the exception of the Italian Renaissance ornamentation around the clock face, all other decoration of the facade was removed during this unfortunate work. On the occasion of the 80th anniversary of the building in 1989, the New York City Landmarks Preservation Commission designated the Metropolitan Life Tower a protected monument. In early 2005 the entire complex was bought by SL Green Realty Corporation. In connection with this first change in ownership in almost 100 years, plans for remodeling the tower levels for residential purposes were made public. As these stories have high ceilings and views that few other sites enjoy, they can be expected to sell for high prices after the renovation.

above: Metropolitan Life
Tower at night
below: Clock with Renaissance
ornamentation

METROPOLITAN LIFE NORTH BUILDING

Entrance portal on Madison Avenue

ADDRESS	STORIES	COMPLETION	HEIGHT	ARCHITECT
11 MADISON AVENUE	29	1933	450 FEET	HARVEY WILEY CORBETT

The Metropolitan Life North Building is an especially illuminating example of the effects of the Great Depression on skyscraper construction during the early 1930s. According to the original plans, this building was intended to have up to 100 stories and a height of approximately 1,300 feet, which would have restored to the Metropolitan Life insurance company the ownership of the tallest building in the world. However, at the height of the Depression this ambitious project came to a halt. What was built instead was a squat, 29-story structure with a height of just 450 feet. The Metropolitan Life North Building did not acquire its present form until the third and, so far, last phase of construction, which ended in 1950. With a gross floor area of 1.9 million square feet, it was one of the largest office blocks in the world at that time. Because of the great depth of the rooms, the lower stories, which have a floor area of over 80,000 square feet, had to be fitted with additional lighting and air-conditioning.

For this gigantic project the architect, Harvey Wiley Corbett, left the committee of architects responsible for the design of the Rockefeller Center (page 150). In his sketches Corbett envisioned a monumental building that, with its wave-shaped profile, would have looked like an enlarged version of the Bank of New York Building (page 20). The base of the Metropolitan Life North Building occupies the entire block of Madison Avenue between 24th Street and 25th Street. Above it is a complex arrangement of setbacks that give the structure the appearance of a telescope with parts that slide into each other. As Corbett designed the facade almost entirely without use of decorative elements, the bulky form of the building is emphasized further.

Even down at street level, three-story round arches at the corners demonstrate the outsize dimensions of the Metropolitan Life North Building. The two lobbies extend along the full length of its axis. They are adorned with coffered ceilings, crossed arches, and gold-veined marble walls. The relatively large number of elevators in these areas is due to the fact that they were planned for the larger number of floors originally intended. This resulted in a benefit for the employees, who could reach their floors without a long wait. Above the two entrance halls there were previously two lower stories that were used for file storage. When the First Boston Investment Bank rented much of the building in 1994, it had the ceiling between these two stories removed, creating a single level with an immense floor area. On its west side the building now accommodates an exclusive restaurant, 11 Madison Avenue, which has a beautiful view of Madison Square Park.

Evening sets in over the Metropolitan Life North Building (left) and the Metropolitan Life Tower.

NEW YORK LIFE BUILDING

(ALSO KNOWN AS NEW YORK LIFE INSURANCE COMPANY BUILDING)

ADDRESS	STORIES	COMPLETION	HEIGHT	ARCHITECT
51 Madison Avenue	40	1928	615 FEET	Cass Gilbert

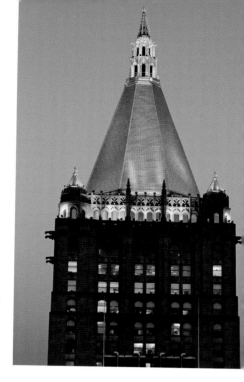

The site today occupied by the New York Life Building has had an eventful history. In the mid-19th century it was still part of the New York Harlem Railroad, until in 1871 the railroad relocated to the area that now holds Grand Central Terminal on 42nd Street. In the following decades the first and later the second Madison Square Garden were located here. No more than three years after the demolition of the multi-purpose arena in 1925, the New York Life Building opened on the site. This was Cass Gilbert's third and final version of a neo-Gothic skyscraper, modeled on his successful West Street Building and Woolworth Building (page 48). The architect succeeded in combining his earlier designs with the forms of 1920s buildings in what was, for a short time, the third-tallest edifice in the world.

The row of monumental high-rise towers stretching along Madison Square Park has a worthy termination in the New York Life Building at the park's northeastern edge. The lower 13 stories of the complex, which was popularly known as the "cathedral of insurance," take up the entire block between 26th Street and 27th Street. A powerful shaft rises above this base, flanked to the east and west up to the height of the 26th story by two building annexes. Decorated arcaded windows, pointed turrets, and Gothic waterspouts characterize the transition to the eight-sided pinnacle, which is covered with gold leaf. At dusk the striking, six-story upper part of the building is magnificently illuminated by spotlights installed below the edge of the roof.

The New York Life Insurance Company intended the conservative style of the building to create associations with its own image of reliability. This aspect of the architecture is reflected in the design of the lobby, where neoclassical-looking lamps are suspended from the vaulted coffered ceiling. A connecting passage also gives employees direct access to the subway station on 28th Street. From its earliest days, the insurance company occupied only the spacious lower floors, while the upper stories were leased to other firms. 50 years after its completion the New York Life Building was included in the National Register of Historic Places. Since 2000, it has enjoyed New York City landmark status.

It is well worth noting the dynamic contrast between different architectural styles displayed on the south side of the building. Here the pale limestone facade and gilded roof of the New York Life Building are reflected on the glass frontage of the Merchandise Mart Building. In spite of this attractive effect, the slab-like skyscraper, completed in 1974 and one of the last typical examples of the International Style, remains an out of place feature on this stretch of Madison Avenue, which takes its character from the three large insurance buildings.

above: Top of the New York Life Building in the evening
below: Total view from the west

EMPIRE STATE BUILDING

ADDRESS	STORIES	COMPLETION	HEIGHT	ARCHITECT
350 Fifth Avenue	102	1931	1,250 feet, (1,472 feet incl. antenna)	William F. Lamb of Shreve, Lamb & Harmon Associates

The Empire State Building is the quintessential skyscraper and remains unmatched in its fame around the world. At its inauguration, New York's new landmark was celebrated as the eighth wonder of the world—a claim that was apt in terms of its technical achievement. With a height of 1,250 feet, it was indisputably the world's tallest building. Its 102 stories and total floor space of 2.3 million square feet also set a new record. At peak periods more than 20,000 people worked in this "vertical city." The 73 elevators were the fastest of their time ("express cars" reach the 80th floor in less than a minute) and the ventilation system pumped a volume of 3.5 million cubic feet of fresh air per minute into the office units.

In the late 1920s, the former chief financial officer of General Motors, John Jacob Raskob, and a former governor of New York, Alfred E. Smith, had envisioned a building that would eclipse everything constructed before it. According to an anecdote, Raskob placed a pencil vertically on the desk and asked the architect, William Lamb, "Bill, how high can you build it so that it won't fall down?" 15 different designs were needed before Lamb decided on the final version. Originally the Empire State Building was to stop at a height of 1,050 feet and surpass the Chrysler Building (page 88), the previous record-holder, by 4 feet. Later an additional 200-feet-high tower was included in the plans, putting a definitive end to the contest over the world's tallest building.

The extremely short construction period of just 13 months was possible because of many innovations to planning, logistics, and design. In addition to the use of prefabricated and standardized constructional elements, all phases of work processes coordinated with one another in an overall organizational scheme. The record speed for performance was 14 new stories erected in only 10 days. In the first half of 1930 alone, 3,400 workers riveted more than 60,000 tons of steel girders. The construction process was recorded by the photographer Lewis Hine, whose book *Men at Work* is an important document of the period. During the Great Depression, an over-supply of workers led to sinking wages. Hence, the construction cost of $42 million ended up being about 20 percent lower than the original estimate.

The Empire State Building stands on a site measuring 410 x 200 feet, which had previously been occupied by the well-known Waldorf=Astoria Hotel. After several setbacks, there is a transition from the base to an elongated shaft at the level of the 30th floor. The centers of its wider north and south facades are opened by recesses that admit increased light into the building's interior. Above the 86th floor rises a slender, gently rounded 16-story tower, which was originally intended as a docking station for dirigibles. Arriving passengers were to be conveyed from here directly to the center of Manhattan (for safety reasons the tower was never used for this purpose). In 1950 a 220-foot-high antenna was added to the top of the building.

The 6,400 windows of the Empire State Building are connected by sheets of shining silver aluminum in addition to the strips of stainless steel that frame them.

View from the north

Seen from street level the building is composed of an abundance of vertical lines that lend a dynamic appearance to its carefully planned design. After dark the set back upper parts are illuminated by more than 500 floodlights. Many variations of color shade can be attained by covering them with disks in 18 different colors.

The multistory entrance hall is designed in classical Art Deco style. In addition to numerous mosaics in metal and marble, a 26-foot-high relief depicts the silhouette of the Empire State Building in aluminum with the rising sun in the background. The lobby is also the starting point for express elevators to the observation deck on the 86th floor, which is open to the public daily from 8:00 a.m. to 2:00 a.m. The observation deck draws more than 3.5 million visitors each year and is one of New York's greatest tourist attractions. At a height of 1,050 feet, it provides a unique 360-degree view of New York and its surroundings (the trip to a second observation deck on the 102nd floor costs extra without really adding a new perspective).

When, on May 1, 1931, President Herbert Hoover officially opened the Empire State Building with the press of button from his office in Washington, D.C., the U.S. economy was in the throes of the Great Depression. Because the building was constructed as speculative office space, most of its floors went unoccupied despite its tremendous prestige. It was not long before the mocking title "Empty State Building" started circulating. Additionally, the number of floors is too high to hold out the prospect of profitable operation, as the utility supply lines and elevator shafts largely swallow up a reasonable level of profit in buildings of this size. As the economy recovered, the empty space was filled up little by little in the mid-1930s, but a reasonable return on the investment was not achieved until the 1950s.

The movie industry was quick to take advantage of the fame of the Empire State Building, which has played a greater or lesser role in more than 100 films. One of the most famous is the 1933 classic *King Kong*. In the closing scenes the giant gorilla fights off attacks by airplanes by swinging at them from the tip of the building. On July 28, 1945, the Empire State Building itself was shaken by the impact of an airplane. On a foggy Sunday morning a B-25 aircraft went off-course and rammed the 79th floor. The pilot and 13 people in the building were killed. Although this was a tragic accident, damage to the building was limited and the following day normal operation was resumed. In the early 1970s, after more than 40 years, the Empire State Building lost its title as the tallest skyscraper to the Twin Towers of the World Trade Center (page 54). In 1981, on the occasion of its 50th anniversary, it was granted landmark status by the City of New York. Five years later, it was awarded the designation of National Historic Landmark. After the collapse of the World Trade Center towers on September 11, 2001, the Empire State Building once again became the tallest building in the city. However, the new buildings at the site of Ground Zero are anticipated to surpass this height when they are completed.

above: View of the building from Fifth Avenue
center: Setbacks in the upper tower
below: Empire State Building in the evening
right: Two New York icons: the Chrysler Building (right)
and the Empire State Building

ONE PENN PLAZA

ADDRESS	STORIES	COMPLETION	HEIGHT	ARCHITECT
250 West 34th Street	55	1972	750 feet	Kahn & Jacobs

One Penn Plaza is one of the many large-scale skyscrapers to appear in major North American cities in the 1960s and 1970s. The exterior design displays the typical characteristics of the International Style. The steel-and-concrete tower has a plateau base that rests on a lot measuring 650 x 200 feet located between 33rd and 34th Street. With a floor area of 85,000 square feet, the lower six stories have the dimensions of a soccer field. By means of two setbacks, the building narrows above the 6th and 11th floors and becomes a slender high-rise slab. It is fronted by a curtain wall of dark-tinted glass, which is subdivided vertically by thin supports of layered aluminum. Although the upper stories taper to a width of only 100 feet at the narrower east and west ends, the floors here have a surface area of 32,000 square feet. With a gross floor area of 2.24 million square feet, it is one of the largest office complexes in Manhattan.

Until the early 1960s, the Beaux-Arts-style buildings of Pennsylvania Station were located on the site adjacent to the south. With ceilings 150 feet high and a waiting room that was 276 feet long, this building of 1910 had similar dimensions to the Grand Concourse of Grand Central Terminal. The demolition of such a magnificent architectural work set off a wave of public protest and was a significant catalyst for the founding of the New York City Landmarks Preservation Commission in 1965. In the course of the enhancement and remodeling of 34th Street in the mid-1990s, major renovation work was also carried out on One Penn Plaza. By polishing the facade and modernizing the interior, the owner aimed to improve the image of the neighborhood and to entice back tenants who had previously moved farther north or to downtown Manhattan.

right: Total view of the building from the east
left: Facade facing 34th Street

NEW YORKER HOTEL

ADDRESS	STORIES	COMPLETION	HEIGHT	ARCHITECT
481 Eighth Avenue	40	1930	470 feet	Sugarman & Berger

"New Yorker" sign on the west facade

Total view of the building from the east

The New Yorker Hotel is one of the most accomplished examples of the setback skyscraper. The six stepped levels above the 20-story base were a result of the New York Zoning Resolution enacted in 1916, which was intended to ensure that future development would still allow enough daylight to reach the street. In contrast to the majority of buildings of its time, the New Yorker Hotel lacks the crowning tower that was often so striking. The vertical indentations at the middle of the facades supply the hotel rooms with maximum light and also to a certain extent relieve the bulky mass of the structure. The neon "New Yorker" signs in large letters on the east and west sides of the roof, which are now once again illuminated when darkness falls, also represent a distinctive feature that is recognizable from afar.

When the $22-million project opened for business on January 2, 1930, its 2,000 rooms made it the largest hotel in the city. During its early years the best big bands of the time performed at the hotel. The kitchen was extremely generously equipped by the standards of the day, with space for 150 cooks. In order to meet the building's enormous demand for power, the basement had its own private generators, providing air-conditioning for all the hotel rooms. With a speed of 800 feet per minute, the elevators held the record for a hotel building; the hairdresser's salon was also the largest in the world when the hotel opened.

After losing money for many years, the hotel was closed in the early 1970s and later used for a variety of other purposes. In 1994 the New Yorker Hotel Management Company bought the building in order to return it to its original purpose after a comprehensive renovation. One by one, the floors of the building were refurbished until by the late 1990s the hotel boasted almost 1,000 newly designed rooms and 100 suites. With its convenient link to Pennsylvania Station to the southeast and immediate proximity to the Jacob K. Javits Convention Center, the location of the New Yorker Hotel, which today belongs to the Ramada group, gives it a significant advantage over the increasing number of other hotels in the city.

AMERICAN RADIATOR BUILDING

(ALSO KNOWN AS AMERICAN STANDARD BUILDING; BRYANT PARK HOTEL)

ADDRESS	STORIES	COMPLETION	HEIGHT	ARCHITECT
40 West 40th Street	22	1924	338 feet	Raymond Hood & André Fouilhoux

Despite its relatively modest height of just 673 feet, the American Radiator Building is one of New York's most important skyscrapers. Its design elements had a direct influence on the subsequent development of high-rise architecture that was equaled by few other buildings. For this building, commissioned by the American Radiator Company, a manufacturer of heating elements and stoves, architect Raymond Hood combined two design proposals from the competition for the Chicago Tribune Tower, which had been held a short time before. On the one hand it incorporates the Gothic tendencies of his own winning entry, while on the other it recalls the skillful massing of Eliel Saarinen's design. In this way the American Radiator Building represents an ideal melding of the two prizewinners of that highly regarded competition. After a construction period of only one year, the 22-story building was completed in 1924. Raymond Hood was one of its first tenants, moving in with his practice to offices on the 14th floor.

Although the majority of architecture critics see the Barclay-Vesey Building (page 52), constructed three years later, as the first Art Deco skyscraper, the American Radiator Building can be considered the first tower to mirror the spirit of the new age. Its black shaft rests on a wide four-story base that occupies the entire site. The adroit composition conceals its function as infill and conveys the impression of a freestanding building. Located opposite the southern boundary of Bryant Park, the building is visible as a whole from the park, where it commands a full view of its elegant structure.

In the preliminary designs for his first tower in New York, Hood noticed that the windows of skyscrapers usually appeared as black holes perforating the shaft. By using black brick as cladding, he made the window openings disappear into their dark surroundings, which created the illusion of a compact, modeled mass. With its chamfered edges and gilded towers, the capital borrows from Gothic architecture. At night, when the lighted windows are set off from the dark shaft and the gilded pinnacle is illuminated by floodlights, the expressive dynamism of the structure is enhanced. Resembling a glowing torch rising above a black mountain of coal— made famous in a 1927 painting by Georgia O'Keeffe— it served as an effective advertisement for the products of the American Radiator Company.

above: View from Bryant Park
center: Entrance on 40th Street
below: Illumination at night

Bronze sheathing and a large showcase window front characterize the building's base, which is clad in black granite. The elaborate ornamentation incorporated above the arched entrance on 40th Street alludes to the transformation of raw materials into energy. Five years after the building was completed, the American Radiator Company merged with the Standard Sanitary Manufacturing Company to form American Standard. In 1937 the newly established corporation installed a display room in the basement for its products. In the late 1990s the office tower was converted into a hotel. As a result of the building's landmark status, only minor changes to the facade were permitted during restoration work. The Bryant Park Hotel, as it is called today, contains 130 rooms of an above-average standard and its basement level boasts of a small theater and the Cellar Bar, featuring vaulted ceilings.

LINCOLN BUILDING

ADDRESS	STORIES	COMPLETION	HEIGHT	ARCHITECT
60 EAST 42ND STREET	53	1930	673 FEET	JOHN E. R. CARPENTER

The Lincoln Building, one of the last New York skyscrapers built in the neo-Gothic style, was completed in 1930 at the intersection of Madison Avenue and 42nd Street. By this time, Art Deco-style towers were already putting their stamp on the cityscape. When it opened, the 53-story office tower was one of the world's tallest buildings. Because of the skillful treatment of massing, a relatively large amount of daylight could reach the office spaces, which led to a reduction in building-operation costs. In addition to the modern features of the building, this fact was a considerable advantage in relation to competing structures along 42nd Street, which were increasing in number around 1930.

The building's massive four-story lower entity extends across the entire site. Above this plateau is a 25-story section marked in its center by a wide recess. At the 29th floor, after four setbacks, the building transforms into a slab-shaped tower. As a result of its elongated plan, the building has relatively sizable square footage on each floor, allowing no work station to be too far from the windows. The vertical positioning of the windows gives the tower slab the appearance of soaring height. Below the edge of the roof they are topped by large pointed Gothic arches.

By the standards of its day the Lincoln Building had a relatively large gross floor area of more than 1.1 million square feet, a result of the spacious floors in the building's base. The lobby is faced with slabs of light brown marble. Expensive chandeliers hang from the lavishly decorated coffered ceiling. Since 1954 a statue of Abraham Lincoln designed by Daniel Chester French—a scaled-down version of the famous sculpture in the Lincoln Memorial in Washington, D.C.—has occupied the center of the lobby. In addition, excerpts from the speeches of the 16th president of the United States can be read on the walls.

above: View from 42nd Street
center: Lincoln statue in the entryway
below: Total view of the building from the north

100 PARK AVENUE

ADDRESS	STORIES	COMPLETION	HEIGHT	ARCHITECT
100 Park Avenue	36	1949	443 feet	Kahn & Jacobs

In the late 1940s, there had been no high-rise construction activity of note for more than 10 years. Although the American economy gradually recovered from the effects of the Great Depression in the mid-1930s, the previous building boom had resulted in an oversupply of office space. It was therefore not until 1949 that a large office building was constructed again in Manhattan. In its shape and facade design 100 Park Avenue, which was sited south of Grand Central Terminal, was based on the functional principles of the International Style and thus differed fundamentally from earlier New York skyscrapers.

New developments made it possible to design the floor plans of this new generation of skyscrapers more efficiently. When it went into operation, 100 Park Avenue was equipped with air-conditioning and fluorescent lighting on all floors. The fluorescent lights that General Electric had produced since 1938 facilitated the large-scale illumination of office areas and made it possible to use a larger amount of floor space. The massive form of the building with its plain facade was to become the standard pattern for most new buildings in the United States constructed during the following years. They had shorter upper towers, whose profitability was more important than achieving prestige through height.

The building at 100 Park Avenue differs from most modern skyscrapers of the 1960s and 1970s in that the bulk of its base is still characterized by its stepped elevation. Above the base section, a 20-story tower slab rises on the east side. Its flat roof was to have groundbreaking significance for future new buildings. Thanks to the large surface of its lower floors, 100 Park Avenue has an impressive gross floor area of 860,000 square feet, in spite of its relatively modest height of 443 feet. The skyscrapers of the 1920s attained a comparable figure only if they were built considerably higher. Moreover, in this new generation of skyscrapers, technical advances meant that almost 80 percent of the total floor space could now be leased to tenants. In comparison to prewar skyscrapers, this represented an increase of around 15 percent.

In early 2008, a major renovation was successfully completed. Through this investment in new design and modern features, an office building that seemed rather colorless in previous years has significantly gained in value and been able to achieve almost 100 percent occupancy of its office space.

above: Total view of the building from the south-east
below: 100 Park Avenue in its urban context before renovation

CHANIN BUILDING

ADDRESS	STORIES	COMPLETION	HEIGHT	ARCHITECT
122 East 42ND Street	56	1929	649 FEET (680 FEET INCL. ROOF STRUCTURES)	SLOAN & ROBERTSON

above: View from 42nd Street
below: The decorative facade on the lower levels

The completion of the Chanin Building was the starting signal for an immense construction boom along 42nd Street. Between 1929 and 1931 a series of outstanding skyscrapers, which to this day are some of the most significant in New York, were built along this heavily used east-west axis. The brisk building activity around Grand Central Terminal highlighted the increasingly strong progression of skyscraper construction toward midtown Manhattan. The neighborhood around 42nd Street now competed directly with the office towers at the southern tip of Manhattan. After the Woolworth Building (page 48) and the Metropolitan Life Tower (page 68), the Chanin Building with its height of 649 feet was for a short time the world's third-highest building. In its massing, it is a mixture of Eliel Saarinen's design for the Chicago Tribune Tower and a rectangular high-rise. In spite of its opulent Art Deco adornment, the slab shape also incorporated at an early date some essential characteristics of the International Style.

Above the ground floor the facade bears a gilded bas-relief showing the evolution of all forms of life, from creatures of the seas and land to birds flying heavenward. A few feet higher a second relief with floral and leaf motifs runs around the building. Both of these works with their typical Art Deco features display a clear rejection of the elements of classical style. Above this, the base of the building narrows in a number of setbacks and at the level of the 32nd floor becomes a slab-shaped shaft that continues into a crown characterized by protruding support beams. At dusk it is floodlit, which makes it even more expressive.

The vertical profile of the structure possesses few decorative elements above the lower stories, but instead embodies in its simplicity a successful interplay of brickwork, metal frames, and tinted glass. By this means the Chanin Building creates a pleasant counterpoint to the works of architecture around Grand Central Terminal that are influenced by Beaux-Arts classicism. The lobby, by contrast, which was designed by Jacques Delamarre and René Chambellan, is less plain, and numbers among the loveliest Art-Deco-style entrance halls. This elongated area bordered by small retail stores features many gilded bronze frames, chandeliers, and screens on the walls without appearing overdecorated. The bronze reliefs entitled *City of Opportunity* and *The Active Life of*

the Individual respectively praise New York as the city of unlimited opportunities, and display the success story of the self-made millionaire Irwin S. Chanin.

The real estate developer, Irwin S. Chanin, was the client for this $14-million project. He established an office and a lavishly designed apartment for his use on the 50th and 51st floors. The prize feature on this level was a bathroom, designed in finest Art Deco style with exclusive Egyptian tiles and expensive paneling, which won a number of awards. Most of the building's gross floor area of 750,000 square feet was occupied by other companies. Proximity to Grand Central Terminal was an essential element in making the building attractive to potential tenants. In the early years there was also a bus station in the basement. Like the little auditorium on the 50th floor and the observation deck directly above it, the bus depot, however, is now closed.

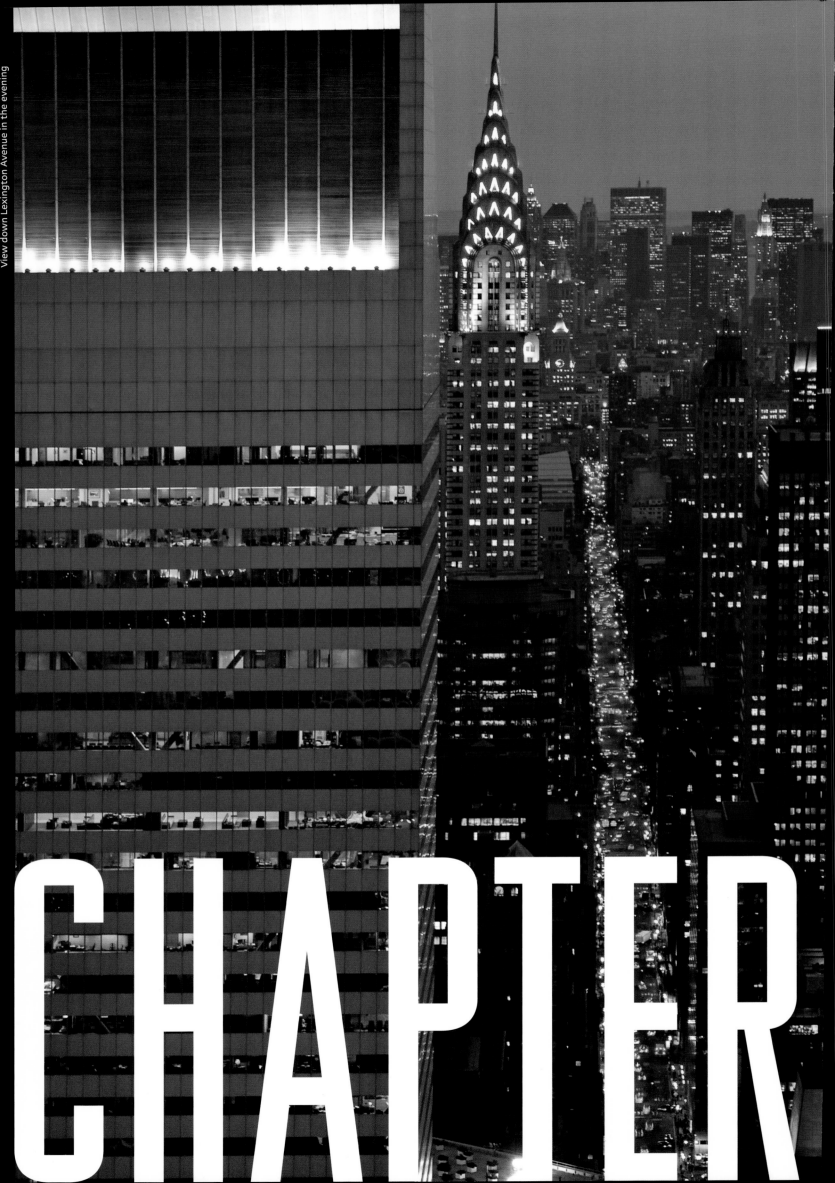

View down Lexington Avenue in the evening

CHAPTER

MIDTOWN EAST

A large proportion of the high-rises found in midtown Manhattan between Lexington Avenue and the East River are characteristic of the International Style. Some of these buildings have had a significant influence on the development of the style, and have made essential contributions to the later ascendancy of modernist architecture. Of particular importance are the Daily News Building and the United Nations Secretariat Building. The Citigroup Center on Lexington Avenue also played an important, if controversial, role. Together with other projects, it ushered in a departure from the orthogonal structures at the end of the 1970s. The area's visual focal point is the Chrysler Building, which uniquely embodies a reach for the skies.

KEY

32	Chrysler Building
33	Daily News Building
34	United Nations Secretariat Building
35	One and Two United Nations Plaza
36	Trump World Tower
37	Beekman Tower Hotel
38	Lipstick Building
39	Bloomberg Tower
40	Citigroup Center
41	General Electric Building
42	Marriott East Side Hotel
43	425 Lexington Avenue

CHRYSLER BUILDING

ADDRESS	STORIES	COMPLETION	HEIGHT	ARCHITECT
405 Lexington Avenue	77	1930	1,046 feet	William Van Allen

No skyscraper reflects the spirit of Art Deco with greater purity and freshness than the Chrysler Building. Having survived myriad changes in taste, its appeal still mirrors the yearnings and aspirations of the 1920s in a singular manner. The tremendous acclaim that has been showered on the Chrysler Building is primarily the result of its extravagant apex, one that expresses an upward soaring in a unique way, endowing the building with an unmistakable identity. A favorite of New Yorkers among Manhattan high-rises, it enjoys unmatched popularity worldwide.

The crucial tower apex in its current form was not a part of the original design and resulted, rather, from an intense personal rivalry in the high-rise construction field. At first, the Chrysler Building—planned for a height of 919 feet—was to have enjoyed the status of the world's tallest building. When its architect, William Van Alen, learned that H. Craig Severance, his former partner, was aiming to build to a height of 927 feet with his Bank of Manhattan Building (page 24), then under construction, Van Alen changed his own plans, adding a 180-foot spire. In August 1930 (three months after the official opening of the Chrysler Building), the so-called "vertex" was lifted into place with a crane in just 90 minutes. Weighing 27 tons, it extended the height of the Chrysler Building to 1,046 feet. This not only made it the world's tallest building; now, it even surpassed the Eiffel Tower in Paris, hitherto the tallest structure ever constructed by human hands. In retrospect, however, this achievement came with a high price, since the smaller upper floors of the Chrysler Building brought little by way of economic advantage. After just one year, moreover, the title of world's tallest building was transferred to the 1,250-foot-high Empire State Building (page 74).

Automobile magnate Walter P. Chrysler was personally in charge of seeing the building scheme through to completion. It was also Chrysler who hired William Van Alen, even though the latter had as yet no reputation as a builder of high-rises. Van Alen's design is conceived in terms of a classical tripartite subdivision into pedestal, shaft, and capital. The building's base has recesses on the east and west sides and is tapered up to the 30th floor in symmetrically arranged setbacks. The facing is brick with gray masonry surrounds. The transition to the shaft is accented by a brick frieze, featuring details representing automobile hubcaps and fenders. Protruding beyond the edges are Mercury's stainless-steel helmets, a then common symbol of the movement and traffic. The middle section of the building rests on a footprint measuring 88 x 108 feet, and rises to the 60th floor. Also faced in brick, the facades are given a pronounced vertical emphasis by prominent supporting pillars. Mounted at the upper edges are eight steel gargoyles, their eagle's heads based on the hood ornament of the 1929 Chrysler Plymouth automobile. Like so many other details, these striking decorative elements were intended to evoke associations with the vehicles manufactured by the automotive company.

The upper section of the building is characterized by its six stainless-steel arches, tapering so that the viewer's gaze is compelled to rise up into the heights. The material used, a chrome-nickel alloy, was at the time new in high-rise construction, and was able to withstand the effects of severe weather. The arches are interrupted by triangular windows that are illuminated at night, endowing the spire with the appearance of an engine hood crowned with spikes.

above: Detail of the building's crown
center: Helmets of Mercury at the transition from the base to the shaft
below: Chrysler Building in its urban context

left: View from the east at night
right: Large steel bird-like decorative elements

During the building's early years the smaller upper floors were occupied by luxury apartments whose windows provided residents with striking views of the cityscape. Formerly located between the 66th and 68th floors was the exclusive "Cloud Club." Decorated with exquisite Art Deco motifs, it long served as an elite club for New York businesspeople. In the spring of 2002, after remaining closed for many years, these floors were converted into office space despite vigorous resistance by the Art Deco Society. The observation deck on the 71st floor was closed as well shortly after it opened since it was unable to compete with the Empire State Building's observation deck.

Located at street level and offering access to the lobby are portals framed in black marble, their design based on the hoods of Chrysler automobiles. Subtly illuminated, the lobby of the building is so elaborately decorated that it resembles a museum of Art Deco design more than it does the entryway to an office high-rise. Elements of this harmonious composition include wall cladding in Moroccan onyx and orange travertine flooring with diagonal metal strips, as well as amber stone ornamentation and various steel elements in zigzag patterns. Hovering above is Edward Trumbull's ceiling painting on the theme of the history of traffic and transportation, which includes a depiction of the Chrysler Building itself. Each of the 32 elevator cabs is lined with expensive wood veneer and accented by elaborate inlays in six different patterns. Today, with a speed of 1,000 feet per minute, these elevators remain among the city's fastest.

In September 1978, the skyscraper—never having actually been used by the Chrysler Corporation as its headquarters—was granted landmark status. Even shortly after its opening, Chrysler occupied only a few of the offices. However, the automotive company did profit from the tremendous acclaim bestowed on this new urban emblem. Even early on, its striking silhouette was used by the advertising and film industries, and the building has retained its unique aura right up to the present day. Especially in the postmodern age, the Chrysler Building has continuously inspired architectural imitations, including Helmut Jahn's design for One Liberty Place in Philadelphia. His 945-foot-high skyscraper is no mere imitation, but instead a respectful tribute to Van Alen's design. In the end, the Chrysler Building not only stands as the high point of Van Alen's career, but also as the beginning of the architect's descent into obscurity. Shortly after the building's completion, Walter P. Chrysler accused Van Alen of accepting bribes in awarding jobs to subcontractors. Although these charges were never substantiated, Van Alen's reputation suffered grievously. Until his death in 1954, William Van Alen would receive no significant further commissions for high-rise designs.

Elevator with elaborate inlay work

DAILY NEWS BUILDING

(ALSO KNOWN AS THE NEWS BUILDING)

Relief above the entrance on 42nd Street

ADDRESS	STORIES	COMPLETION	HEIGHT	ARCHITECT
220 EAST 42ND STREET	36	1930	475 FEET	RAYMOND HOOD AND JOHN MEAD HOWELLS

In the late 1920s, when the New York Daily News (a subsidiary of the Chicago Tribune) decided to construct a new headquarters building, the commission went to architects Raymond Hood and John Mead Howells. Just a few years earlier, this team had been responsible for the winning design for Chicago's Tribune Tower. The two architects reprised their partnership for this new project, creating a building that broke radically with the high-rise construction of the preceding decades. In fact, the Daily News Building represents the real birth of the slab-style high-rise. Rejected now was the conventional structural formula consisting of a wide pedestal topped by a shaft and terminating in a pointed apex or pyramid. (In an allusion to its owner, the building was often compared to a tall vertical stack of newspapers.)

The most important structural change was the replacement of the frequently seen stepped form with an ornamental crown by a vertical, undecorated brick slab, one whose terraced setbacks, now greatly reduced in number, were restrained and meticulously configured. Set between load-bearing elements are vertically arranged strip windows; these are interrupted by red and black brick surrounds whose effect is sculptural in character. The fenestration is slightly recessed as a result, which gives the facade the form of a relief. This loosened slab form also allowed the office levels to be used with greater efficiency. These were arranged in such a way that no workplace was set more than 27 feet from a window. From the beginning, only the lower floors were occupied by the newspaper's offices. The upper floors were designed as speculative office space. This plan was somewhat risky, as the Daily News Building was located east of Third Avenue, apart from the high-rise development occurring at the time.

Set above the entry area on 42nd Street was a three-story relief depicting American office workers in lavish detail. At the center of the relief is an image of the Daily News Building, set before a rising sun. The focal point of the Art Deco lobby is a large, slowly revolving globe that sinks down into the terrazzo floor, symbolizing the international outlook of the newspaper, with the dark, faceted cupola rising above it embodying the infinite

beyond. 30 years after its completion, the Daily News Building was expanded to include a pair of additions on its east and south sides, whose exteriors were designed to harmonize with the facade of the main building. The flatter nine-story unit to the south served as a new space for the printing presses, while the 18-story eastern unit consisted entirely of offices. The total available floor area of the complex was nearly doubled and now amounts to more than 1.1 million square feet.

Many critics and historians regard the Daily News Building as the first classic modernist skyscraper. In 1981 the building was granted landmark status in recognition of its enormous contribution to high-rise building. With the completion of Rockefeller Center (page 150), whose buildings are similar in many respects to the Daily News Building, its far-reaching influence was evident to all. The New York Daily News remained faithful to "its" skyscraper until the mid-1990s, when it relocated and the structure was officially renamed the "News Building." Many film buffs recognize it as the "Daily Planet Building" from the Superman movies.

Globe in the lobby

UNITED NATIONS SECRETARIAT BUILDING

ADDRESS	STORIES	COMPLETION	HEIGHT	ARCHITECT
405 EAST 42ND STREET	39	1952	505 FEET	COMMITTEE OF INTERNATIONAL ARCHITECTS, CHAIR: WALLACE K. HARRISON

The United Nations complex extends from 42nd to 48th Street on an 18-acre site that runs along the East River. John D. Rockefeller purchased the plot in December 1945 for $8.5 million and bequeathed it to the United Nations (U.N.), the global peace-keeping organization that had been founded slightly earlier in San Francisco. As an international territory, it belongs neither to New York City nor to the United States. Two years after the site was purchased, a committee of international architects came together to plan its development. The plan chosen comes closest to the design "23 A" by the Swiss-born architect Le Corbusier. It served as a general master plan for the construction of the United Nations complex, whose most striking structure is the Secretariat Building.

The exterior design of the 39-story skyscraper consists of an unmodulated upright slab free of setbacks and ornamentation. The windowless facades of the north and south sides, just 80 feet wide, are clad in white Vermont marble. Far more spectacular are the eastern and western facades, almost 280 feet wide, which made this the first high-rise office building to feature a glass curtain wall. In conjunction with a dense network of metal paneling, the turquoise-tinted windows form a single plane with the surface of the facade. With its crisp form and glazed curtain wall, the Secretariat Building would become the prototypical International Style skyscraper. The building renounces all the external decoration, opting instead for a linear shape.

Design disagreements over the building's execution prompted Le Corbusier to withdraw from the project. He was replaced by Wallace K. Harrison. In order to mitigate the heating effect of solar radiation, thermopane glass was inserted into the facade. Despite this measure, energy consumption rose to extremely high levels (although at the time, conserving was not yet an issue of pressing urgency). The concealed support pillars are set at intervals of 28 feet, and subdivide the wide facades into 10 vertical units. The self-supporting, unified glass wall is suspended in front, giving the building a pronounced horizontal emphasis. Later, Le Corbusier, would ridicule the glazed outer skin, remarking that it resembled a cellophane wrapper. Other critics found that the interconnected character of the various architectural elements of the United Nations was thrust into the background by the powerful appearance of the U.N. Secretariat Building. The building came to symbolize the different divisions of the United Nations, with the headquarters building standing prominently in the foreground, while the Assembly Building, with its windowless walls, lay metaphorically at its feet.

Despite criticisms of its excessively large scale in relationship to the surrounding structures, the Secretariat Building represents a milestone in the development of high-rise architecture. In fall 2007, long-overdue and highly expensive renovations were begun throughout the complex. These will include in particular the removal of asbestos and lead and the installation of a hitherto absent sprinkler system. For the time being, visitors can still enjoy free guided tours of the Assembly Building (daily from 9:30 a.m. to 4:45 p.m.). The United Nations Park, which adjoins the complex to the north offers a remarkable collection of artworks designed to give visual expression to the desire for world peace.

above: View of the United Nations from the north side
right: *Non Violence* sculpture by Fredrik Reuterswärd

ONE AND TWO UNITED NATIONS PLAZA

ADDRESS	STORIES	COMPLETION	HEIGHT	ARCHITECT
1 AND 2 UNITED NATIONS PLAZA	39	1975 (ONE UNITED NATIONS PLAZA) 1981 (TWO UNITED NATIONS PLAZA)	505 FEET	KEVIN ROCHE, JOHN DINKELOO & ASSOCIATES

The two towers of One and Two United Nations Plaza, which stand at right angles to one another, are parts of the large-scale western extension of the United Nations. Although six years separated the completion of the first from the second building, they have always conveyed the impression of a close-knit unity. Seen close-up, their extraordinary identical geometric forms are an almost

vertiginous sight. The incised edges of their lower sections and the slanted setbacks visible in the upper third of each structure deprive the buildings of a sense of static solidity. Each structure features the glass curtain wall characteristic of architectural modernism as a whole, but their departure from the right angle is a trait typical of the late-modernist high-rise. While this feature anticipates the postmodernist tendency that would emerge subsequently, their rejection of facade decoration testifies to their fidelity to a modernist aesthetic.

Both towers are clad in a uniform gridded skin of mirrored turquoise-tinted glass. This choice of facade design not only emphasizes the extraordinary forms of these buildings, but also generates a colorist dialogue with the United Nations Secretariat Building (page 94), and is a striking example of the way in which an abstract building can make direct reference to adjoining structures. The mirrored glass cladding reflects the surroundings without affording views into the interiors. An additional disorienting factor is the use of panes of glass measuring only 5 x 3 feet, subdivided by white-coated aluminum strips, which do not correspond to the divisions of the stories. This impression of a lack of coherent scale is heightened even further by the extraordinary volumes of the buildings. Given their immediate proximity to the United Nations complex, they were not permitted to surpass the height of the U.N. Secretariat Building. At 505 feet, they are exactly the same height as the Secretariat Building, and each has the same number of stories—39. Organizationally, they are designed to accommodate mixed use; the lower 26 stories consist exclusively of office levels, while the upper 12 stories of each building contain the facilities of the Millennium UN Plaza Hotel.

above: Bridge connecting the two towers
left: Total view of the building from the east

TRUMP WORLD TOWER

ADDRESS	STORIES	COMPLETION	HEIGHT	ARCHITECT
845 United Nations Plaza	72	2001	862 feet	Costas Kondylis & Associates

Since 2001 the Turtle Bay neighborhood has been dominated by the massive Trump World Tower. When completed, the Tower—a skyscraper located northwest of the
United Nations and boasting a height of 862 feet—was
the world's tallest purely residential building and New
York's tallest new structure in 24 years. According to its
detractors, the splashy project violated both area building codes and tradition. These were based on, among
other things, an agreement whereby no building in the
immediate vicinity of the United Nations would be allowed to overtake the Secretariat Building (page 94) in
height. In the end, expensive legal proceedings resulted
in the rejection of these complaints by a New York court.

Before the $400-million project could be realized in
its current form, air rights had to be acquired and transferred as a package to the new development. The mono-
lithic skyscraper rises without setbacks to a height of
72 stories. Its 374 lavishly designed luxury apartments
are distributed throughout a floor area of more than
800,000 square feet. Ceiling heights range from 10 feet
in the lower stories, to just 16 feet in the penthouses,
which feature fireplaces. As a result of a framing concrete girdle, all residential units enjoy good acoustic and
thermal insulation. In order to allow the strikingly slim
tower to resist strong lateral winds, it was provided with
additional strengthening elements. Besides the concrete
girdle around the building's midsection, these include a
heavy roof element. This "concrete tunnel" as a whole is
masked by a concealing bronze curtain wall.

Residents—including such celebrities as Bill Gates,
Sophia Loren, and Harrison Ford—enjoy the use of a
fitness facility with adjoining swimming pool, a first-
class restaurant, and underground garage, as well as
round-the-clock concierge services. For residents of the
adjacent buildings, however, this project was anything
but a boon. Apart from the enormous shadows it cast,
this tall tower restricts views from neighboring office and
residential buildings, thereby diminishing their value to a
considerable degree.

above: View from the
United Nations Park
right: Trump World Tower
in its urban context

BEEKMAN TOWER HOTEL
(FORMERLY THE PANHELLENIC TOWER)

ADDRESS	STORIES	COMPLETION	HEIGHT	ARCHITECT
3 Mitchell Place	26	1928	288 feet	John Mead Howells

With his Panhellenic Tower (now the Beekman Tower Hotel), completed in 1928, John Mead Howells demonstrated yet again his standing as one of the most creative architects of the 1920s. While his tower, which is incised at the corners, reaches a height of just 300 feet, its severe lines already anticipate tendencies of the following generation of high-rises. The building's outward appearance resembles a simplified version of the American Radiator Building (page 80). That skyscraper, completed just a few years earlier, had similar dimensions, and was a further development of Chicago's Tribune Tower, designed by Hood and Howells. With the Panhellenic Tower, this trilogy acquires a worthy terminus, and demonstrates impressively the transition from the decorative classical style to the simpler forms favored in the ensuing years.

The vertical structures of the facades are formed by deeply recessed and enclosed tiers of windows set between massive supporting pillars. The 26-story tower almost entirely rejects the decorative elements typical of the time. Only the rounded windows at the lower stories and the ornamentation above are an exception to this. The tower's expressiveness and power, finally, are a function of the sheer dynamism of its upwardly soaring supporting and window elements. Seen from an extreme angle, the windows disappear entirely behind the pillars, creating the illusion of an enormous wall of stone. A good 30 years later, in his CBS Building (page 154), Eero Saarinen, too, would exploit such a design strategy, recessing tiers of windows behind triangular pillars.

Above the 19th floor, the building's footprint is reduced in a series of gently terraced setbacks. The tapering form in the upper third of the building was not a concession to the building ordinances, but instead served simply to loosen up the appearance of the whole. At the same time, it gave an impression of greater height. The crown-like upper terminus contains an open arcade behind which are the mechanical installations. At the 26th floor, is the "Top of the Tower" restaurant. Its extensive exterior glazing offers diners panoramic views onto the East River and the development around the United Nations.

In its early years, the Panhellenic Tower served as a residential hotel for young women belonging to national Greek-letter sororities. Under the name "Beekman Tower Hotel," it later became a fine-quality hotel. 70 years after its completion, it was designated a city landmark. The New York City Landmarks Preservation Commission gave as its reasons the fact that the tower's forward-looking design exercised a strong influence on later developments in high-rise construction.

above: View of the building from the north-west.
below: Entrance at Mitchell Place

LIPSTICK BUILDING

(ALSO KNOWN AS 885 THIRD AVENUE)

ADDRESS	STORIES	COMPLETION	HEIGHT	ARCHITECT
885 THIRD AVENUE	34	1986	453 FEET	JOHNSON & BURGEE

With its unconventional oval shape, the so-called "Lipstick Building" departs from the uniformly rectangular development along Third Avenue, loosening-up the narrow, rectilinear grid of the block. In contrast to the neighboring office buildings, the majority of which were erected during the 1960s and 1970s, there is no street-front plaza. The elliptical form of the building automatically creates open areas that provide pedestrians with additional space in the often overflowing streets. The rounded facade is formed by stacked bands of enameled pink-painted granite, strips of reflective stainless steel, and gray-tinted windowpanes and is otherwise free of ornamentation. The two telescopic reductions of the building's diameter on the west side, however, were not based on aesthetic considerations but instead were necessary in order to comply with building codes.

Shortly after this office building became occupied, its original identification as simply "885 Third Avenue" faded away. Due to the exceptional public interest prompted by its extraordinary design, it soon became familiar under the sobriquet the "Lipstick Building." Not unlike the Flatiron Building (page 66), it acquired its official name by virtue of its external shape. But it has also evoked a number of additional associations. A few observers were reminded of the smokestack of an ocean liner, while for others, the Lipstick Building resembles a stack of movie reels. The non-standardized footprint entailed higher costs than a conventional office building. Besides the need to fit heating, ventilation, and air-conditioning equipment into its shape, the subdivision of the office units had to be adapted to the oval shape of the level. For this reason, the core shaft—which contains the elevator units—was not centrally positioned, but is instead located on the rear east side, which has no setbacks.

The luxurious if restrained detailing is typical of designs by Philip Johnson and John Burgee. The team's talent for staging unusual building forms, thereby providing welcome relief from the regularity of New York's high-rise jungle had been certified two years earlier with the emphatic exclamation point that is the AT&T Building (page 136). Its design is an impressive instance of the then emergent, highly visionary, and aesthetic tendencies of postmodernist architecture. In particular the use of stainless steel as a facade material on the Lipstick Building established a link to the skyscrapers of the Art Deco age, and satisfied yearnings for the well-designed buildings of that era. At the same time, the oval shape clarified a new conception of architectural contour, emphasizing that the exterior design of the skyscraper remained in a constant state of development. In a certain sense, Philip Johnson (who maintained an office in the building until the mid-1990s) repudiated his own past with his postmodernist designs. For it was Johnson who in 1932 had asserted that high-rise architecture was not built sculpture.

above: View of the east facade without setbacks
left: Lipstick Building in its urban context

BLOOMBERG TOWER

(ALSO KNOWN AS 1 BEACON COURT; 731 LEXINGTON AVENUE)

ADDRESS	STORIES	COMPLETION	HEIGHT	ARCHITECT
731 Lexington Avenue	54	2005	806 feet (941 feet incl. antenna mast)	Cesar Pelli & Associates

Bloomberg Tower is among the best regarded works of architecture produced in New York in recent years. When the $450-million project opened its doors after nearly four years of construction activity, it occupied the entire city block lying between 58th and 59th Street. The complex consists of two contrasting structures: a tall, towering building on Lexington Avenue, and a squatter unit toward the east. While both its vast glass surfaces and its form, characterized by right angles, are classically modernist in nature, the tower's stepped form is reminiscent of the skyscrapers of the Art Deco age. The building's mixed use exerted an influence on the load-bearing structure. The office levels found in the lower 30 stories are carried by a steel skeleton, while the residential units above were given a concrete frame. Depending upon size, the 105 spacious luxury apartments fetched prices ranging from $5 to $30-million.

In addition to office and residential units, early plans also envisioned a luxury hotel for the middle section of the tower. When the future principal tenant, Bloomberg Financial News Service, doubled its required office area to 700,000 square feet, plans for the hotel had to be scrapped. With more than 4,000 employees, the new main headquarters of the stock information service, founded in 1982, is also the only tenant in the office levels of Bloomberg Tower. Adjoining the tower to the east is a flat, eight-storied unit. It extends around an oval-shaped inner courtyard whose west side accommodates the entrance to the residences of 1 Beacon Court. Rising around this atrium are the glass-clad facade fronts of a 160,000 square feet row of offices and shops, where the top-flight restaurant "Le Cirque" opened in June of 2006. At sundown, the glass fronts begin to glow in a variety of tones, rendering this area even more powerfully expressive than during the daytime.

At 806 feet, the Bloomberg Tower is the most prominent building in the northeastern part of Midtown Manhattan. Among the city's most coveted, the apartments in the upper stories offer unobstructed views onto Central Park and broad areas of Midtown. The building's slender form makes it relatively susceptible to the effects of wind forces. In order to overcome this problem, a dual vibration damper system was installed in the roof construction, reducing vibration amplitude by around 50 percent. The mixed use of the complex, with office, residential, and retail units, integrates it seamlessly into the urban context. Especially notable is the Bloomingdales department store - one of the city's largest and best-known - adjoining the complex on the north side. New York City's land-use ordinance fostered the mixed-use character of new buildings in that it afforded the construction project an increase in overall floor space of about 20 percent. Nevertheless, it required the acquisition of air rights from neighboring buildings to gain permission to build the 1.3 million square feet of gross floor area.

above: View from the west
right: Courtyard in the evening hours

CITIGROUP CENTER

(ALSO KNOWN AS CITICORP CENTER)

ADDRESS	STORIES	COMPLETION	HEIGHT	ARCHITECT
153 EAST 53RD STREET	59	1977	915 FEET	HUGH STUBBINS & ASSOCIATES, EMERY ROTH & SONS

Like no other building from the 1970s, the Citigroup Center set the stage for the sweeping changes and new expectations that characterized the latest generation of skyscrapers. At the same time, it symbolized New York City's return to a position of strength after one of its most severe economic crisis. Breaking with the right angles of the International Style, it smoothed the way for the emergence of postmodernist architecture. A number of critics have regarded it as the first skyscraper of this stylistic era—one that (as a result of the building recession of the 1970s) flowered fully only in the following decade. Even today, more than 30 years after its completion, the Citigroup Center's sharply sloping roof and height of 915 feet make it an outstanding monument on the New York skyline. In its unorthodox massing, it summarizes the best tendencies of the period while avoiding an impression of severity through its asymmetrical angles.

In addition to its nearly 160-foot-tall roof, the pedestal is also a source of much public attention. The tower as a whole rests on a quartet of powerful, 115-foot-tall pillars, as well as a central shaft. The raising of the building to a height of approximately 10 stories created an open surface below. With seating and planted areas, this plaza—set several feet below street level—is publicly accessible. In contrast to the sterile plazas that appear in front of many high-rises, it has become popular with the public and affords the rare opportunity to linger comfortably below a skyscraper.

In building the new headquarters for Citibank, the architect, Hugh Stubbins, wanted to erect an artistic highlight. In addition to diverging from typical high-rise typologies in its upper and lower zones, his building was also designed to be distinctive with regard to conventional standards of surface design. The cladding, consisting of uniform alternating layers of reflective glass and coated aluminum, lends the facade a strongly expressive character. Behind the facade are diagonal braces, each extending to a length of more than eight stories. Intended to divert the impact of gale-force winds into the powerful pillars, these provide the load-bearing frame with greater stability.

A precondition for the authorization of this project was that St. Peter's Lutheran Church—which had stood on the northwestern end of the site since 1862—had to be rebuilt at the same location. The church's small congregation received more than $9 million for the sale of the building's air rights alone. An additional requirement made by the congregation was that despite the presence of its far larger neighboring building, the church would be able to retain its own identity and maintain an unobstructed view of the sky. In order to satisfy these requirements the decision was made to elevate the Citigroup building on a tall supporting structure and to position it along the southern boundary of the site. The church— clad in gray granite paneling—occupies approximately one-third of the site's surface area, its rectangular form harmonizing with the adjacent architecture.

above: View from the north-west
below: Sunken plaza on Lexington Avenue

Until the early 1970s, energy conservation played no significant role in high-rise planning. Only after the oil crisis was serious consideration given to the environmental aspects of planning and to their economic implications. It was this new sense of responsibility that led Citigroup Center to be the first skyscraper to install systems designed to minimize energy use. Among these measures were energy saving lamps and a recycled-heating system. The installation of space-saving double-deck elevators reverted to an innovation introduced in the early 1930s. Perhaps the most spectacular proposal for the exploitation of alternative energy sources envisioned the mounting of solar collectors on the slanting roof surface. With its energy capacity, the air-conditioning system was to have run the entire complex. These considerations were never actually implemented—any more than the original plan for accommodating residential units in the attic stories.

Apart from the mechanical installations located in the lower levels of the roof structure, the ultimate use of the roof space remained unclear during construction. This question was quickly resolved when the engineer responsible for the structure, William LeMessurier, based on an observation made by a student, identified an alarming circumstance in his post-construction calculations. Due to the building's relatively minimal deadweight, and to its particular construction form, which transferred the greater part of the total load to the four main supporting pillars, the building was subject to excessive swaying when exposed to high winds. Theoretically, hurricane-strength could even have caused the skyscraper to collapse. In order to counteract these dangerous oscillations, Le Messurier had a 400-ton, 30-foot square concrete block installed in the roof. The Citigroup Center tuned mass damper—the first ever installed in a high-rise—was based on the principle of mass inertia. Guided by sensors, and gliding on oiled tracks, it is capable of responding within a fraction of a second to compensate for up to 50 percent of the building's oscillations. In addition to the installation of a tuned mass damper (a concept applied to many high-rise projects since), was the welding together of the steel plates of the diagonal struts, formerly connected by means of rivets. This stiffening provides the building with greater resistance to the stresses created by oblique wind forces.

Aligned with the eastern edge of the site is a seven-story atrium. With a surface area of 210,000 square feet, it accounts for approximately one-seventh of the gross floor area of the entire complex. Surrounded by shops and restaurants, the 80-foot-high atrium features plantings and café tables. On the west side, a gigantic load-bearing pillar of the office tower forms a spectacular backdrop. One block south of Citigroup Center, 599 Lexington Avenue represents one of the best examples of postmodernist architecture's attempt to enter into a dialogue with its surrounding structures. The angular form of the 653-foot-tall office building focuses on establishing a visual link to Citigroup Center completed 10 years previously. One positive side effect of these efforts has been the enriching of the New York City skyline with an additional novel element. When standing between these buildings and gazing upward into the sky, visitors enjoy spectacular perspectives formed by the contrasting geometric shapes of the two buildings.

left: View from Lexington Avenue towards the sky
right: Citigroup Center and 599 Lexington Avenue (right)

GENERAL ELECTRIC BUILDING

(NOW 570 LEXINGTON AVENUE)

ADDRESS	STORIES	COMPLETION	HEIGHT	ARCHITECT
570 LEXINGTON AVENUE	50	1931	640 FEET	CROSS & CROSS

In outward appearance, the General Electric (G.E.) Building—completed in 1931—has much in common with the skyscrapers of the 1920s. Yet its design, rather than representing a retreat to the preceding decade, instead succeeds at a respectful integration into the existing urban context. In this 50-story skyscraper, the architectural firm of Cross & Cross attempted to unite two divergent elements: first, 20th-century technology, and second, the forms of medieval architecture. This second aspect was primarily intended to establish a harmonious relationship with the neighboring St. Bartholomew Church on Park Avenue. For this reason, the General Electric Building uses exclusively materials and colors that are compatible with the Byzantine style of the church's exterior. The outcome of these constraints is one of New York City's most elegant high-rises. This avoids allowing the far smaller church to be crushed by the new and far more massive

structure and prevents the larger building from becoming an oversized solitary entity.

The most memorable feature of the General Electric Building is the patterned masonry tracery at its apex. With its mixture of pointed towers and brickwork decorations, it is reminiscent of traditional Gothic towers. Its zigzag lines were also intended as allusions to abstract representations of radio waves. These details are emblematic of the building's principal tenant, the Radio Corporation of America (RCA), which occupied most of the office floors. In addition to numerous further ornamental details, each side of the crown is decorated by two-storied sculptures portraying American Indians. After sunset, the building's apex is illuminated by floodlights, causing it to resemble an enormous torch.

At street level, the facades along Lexington Avenue and 51stStreet are decorated with stainless-steel Art Deco motifs and simplified models of the tower. The units above are clad in brown and orange brickwork. After a number of terraced recessions, the pedestal narrows above the 25th story into a slender shaft whose corners have been sliced away. The vertical window strips are subdivided by slightly protruding pillars. Set between the windows are elaborately decorated railing elements. The lobby was designed with an equal attention to detail. In addition to its silver-plated sun motifs are Art Deco lamps, whose aquamarine tinted glass provides the space with understated illumination.

Not long after the building's inauguration, RCA, the original client, moved its headquarters to Rockefeller Center (page 150). The new tenant of the building was the General Electric Company. In the 1980s, after G.E. also moved to Rockefeller Center, the building's name was changed to "570 Lexington Avenue." Yet in the popular consciousness, the building remains associated with the giant conglomerate that maintained its New York headquarters here for so many years. In the mid-1990s, the skyscraper was donated to Columbia University, which immediately undertook an award-winning restoration. After its completion, in 1998 the General Electric Building was granted landmark status by the New York City Landmarks Preservation Commission.

above: Facade decoration as seen from the street
left: View from the north-east

MARRIOTT EAST SIDE HOTEL

(FORMERLY THE SHELTON TOWERS HOTEL; HALLORAN HOUSE)

Entrance on Lexington Avenue

ADDRESS	STORIES	COMPLETION	HEIGHT	ARCHITECT
525 Lexington Avenue	32	1924	388 feet	Arthur Loomis Harmon

The Shelton Towers Hotel (now, the Marriott East Side Hotel), completed in 1924, was the first New York setback skyscraper which fully exploited the requirements of the Zoning Resolution of 1916. Now, the average citizen could gauge exactly the impact of the new building regulations. To be sure, other buildings erected in New York in the preceding years had been subject to the new regulations, but none had possessed the typical stepped character of this new generation of high-rise.

The building achieves its powerful impact less through elaborate ornamentation than through its massing. This was explored in Hugh Ferriss's celebrated charcoal drawings from the early 1920s—perspectival renderings used by this architectural draftsman to illustrate the possibilities of New York City's building codes. The brown brick facade of the Marriott East Side Hotel formed an uninterrupted surface that guides the gaze toward the sculptural contours of the setbacks and their cornices. Only the two lower and two upper stories, with their pale limestone cladding and round arched windows, deviate from the building's otherwise uniform profile.

When it opened, the 1,200 rooms of the Shelton Towers Hotel made it the largest hotel in the world. In the beginning, it also accommodated a fitness center with solaria, squash courts, and a swimming pool. In the course of time, however, these facilities made way for increasing numbers of guestrooms. Because of the rising public interest in the real estate of midtown Manhattan, the hotel soon came to be favored as a permanent residence by celebrities, including the painter Georgia O'Keeffe and her husband, the photographer Alfred Stieglitz. These artists painted and photographed the surrounding buildings visible from their apartment on the 28th floor. Their images circulated throughout the world, and continue to constitute valuable historical testimony today. As early as the building boom of the late 1920s, and with the arrival in the immediate vicinity of markedly larger luxury hotels such as the Waldorf=Astoria (page 122), the Shelton Towers Hotel gradually lost its prominence on Lexington Avenue. Extensive renovations were undertaken in 1978, and this four-star hotel now has approximately 650 rooms.

Total view of the building from the south

425 LEXINGTON AVENUE

ADDRESS	STORIES	COMPLETION	HEIGHT	ARCHITECT
425 LEXINGTON AVENUE	31	1987	411 FEET	HELMUT JAHN

By the early 1980s, the innovative designs of the German-American architect Helmut Jahn (born in Nuremberg in 1940, he has lived in Chicago for many years) had earned him a substantial reputation. A little later in the decade, he attracted attention in New York with incisive designs, including one for 425 Lexington Avenue. With this 31-story office tower, the architect achieved a difficult balancing act, integrating a postmodern building seamlessly into a district characterized by Art Deco skyscrapers and International Style high-rises. Jahn sought to generate a visual relationship with the adjacent buildings, not by imitating them, but instead by emphasizing the most salient characteristics of each one. The building at 425 Lexington Avenue is not only one of the architect's best works; it is also a premier exemplar of the post-modernist high-rise.

With its tripartite division, consisting of a distinctive base, a uniform shaft, and a roof with a jutting cornice, the structure assumes the form of a classical column. Its crown-like upper terminus is formed on three sides by a slightly projecting, three-story-high unit that contains office conference rooms. Sliced off at the corners, the shaft is octagonal in outline. Its turquoise glazed sheathing engages in a dialogue with the neighboring International Style glass towers.

A special challenge was posed by the immediate proximity of the Chrysler Building (page 88). The unenviable task of erecting a skyscraper just one block north of this iconic structure was solved by Jahn with impressive skill. On the one hand, his office tower is contextual with the Chrysler Building; on the other, it has an independent profile. Its reflective surface bespeaks admiration for its celebrated neighbor, which is literally mirrored in the Jahn building. The mild distortions resulting from this gesture underline once again the extraordinary verve of 425 Lexington Avenue. The projecting capital, found at approximately the same height as the protruding elements on the lower shaft of the Chrysler Building, are by no means an attempt to compete with the apex of that structure. Instead, the effect is of a delicate symbiosis between contrasting buildings.

Total view of the building taken from the east

Facade with overhanging window cornices

CHAPTER

NORTH OF GRAND CENTRAL TERMINAL

The area north of Grand Central Terminal is among the most expensive real estate in Manhattan, and one of the most densely populated with high-rises. Its numerous subway lines have always had a strong influence on the foundations of neighborhood skyscrapers. Set along Park Avenue is a mixture of buildings representing the most diverse stylistic tendencies. In the Seagram Building and Lever House, the best and most significant examples of the International Style are found. With its massive form, the MetLife Building (formerly the Pan Am Building), which rises above Grand Central Terminal, also serves as a vivid example of the kind of architecture that would later discredit this stylistic phase. Perhaps the greatest masterpiece of the subsequent postmodernist age is the AT&T Building (now the Sony Building), sited a few blocks farther northwest on Madison Avenue. As a result of the enormous public interest that greeted its completion, it made a substantial contribution to the positive transformation of New York's skyline in the 1980s.

KEY

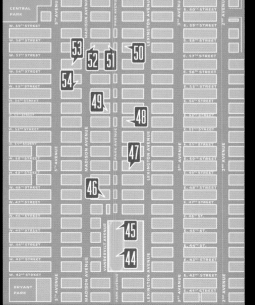

44   **MetLife Building**

45   **Helmsley Building**

46   **Union Carbide Building**

47   **Waldorf–Astoria Hotel**

48   **Seagram Building**

49   **Lever House**

50   **Ritz Tower**

51   **Four Seasons Hotel**

52   **Fuller Building**

53   **IBM Building**

54   **AT&T Building**

5

METLIFE BUILDING
(FORMERLY PAN AM BUILDING)

ADDRESS	STORIES	COMPLETION	HEIGHT	ARCHITECT
200 Park Avenue	59	1963	808 feet	Emery Roth & Sons, Pietro Belluschi, Walter Gropius

View from the south

The MetLife Building (formerly the Pan Am Building) is one of Manhattan's first mega buildings. While monumental International Style architectural complexes continued to be built well into the 1970s, no New York high-rise project before or after unleashed such a storm of protest. Its massive volume is a paradigm of failed urban planning, and testifies to the utter recklessness with which the metropolitan context was approached at that time. It came as no surprise when a survey carried out in 1987 showed that New Yorkers named the Pan Am Building as the one they would most like to see torn down.

The original plans of the architectural firm of Emery Roth & Sons had the office tower's lengthwise axis running north to south. The architects Walter Gropius und Pietro Belluschi, who joined the project later, rotated the structure by 90 degrees. Now, the building's facade, more than 300 feet wide, blocked views along Park Avenue. Gropius was also responsible for the departure from the then customary glass facade. In his view, a glass-clad building of such dimensions would lack solidity. Yet its prefabricated concrete elements only serve to underscore an impression of bulkiness, demonstrating that a repudiation of the glass-box model does not automatically solve all problems.

With a gross floor area of nearly 3.2 million square feet (2.8 million square feet of which are leasable), the Pan Am Building was for nine years the largest office building in the world. In conjunction with its central location and excellent transportation connections, the generous floor area guaranteed that just three months after its inauguration, almost 90 percent of the office space would be leased. Approximately one quarter of this space was originally occupied by Pan American Airways.

The lowest element of the building consists of a 10-story base that extends from 43rd to 45th Street and encompasses a surface area of more than 100,000 square feet. Its visual merging with the cornice of Grand Central Terminal, built in 1913, constitutes an especially graphic instance of the insensitive treatment of the architectural context. The office tower rising above the space has an elongated octagonal plan. With its converging flanks, it has the appearance of an upright hydrofoil. The modi-

fication of the originally rectangular slab was the work of Emery Roth & Sons. This, however, was not meant to refer to Pan Am, the building's principal tenant, but was intended instead to relieve the structure of some of its massiveness. At the 22nd and 47th stories, the surfaces of the facades are interrupted by loggias. Located behind these is the mechanical equipment, accommodated here because the tower lacks basement levels. Set below the roofline on the north and south sides are two double-height MetLife logos.

The building's base enjoys direct access to the concourse level of Grand Central Terminal. In order to facilitate navigating the streams of commuters, Gropius opted for a network of 14 escalators that provided access to the mezzanine. From this point, employees are conveyed by 59 passenger elevators directly to the office tower (the large number of elevators ensures a maximum wait of 12 seconds). The various entry areas feature numerous artworks, among them Richard Lippold's brass-wire sculpture *Flight*, installed in the Vanderbilt Avenue lobby.

Shortly after the inauguration of the Pan Am Building, a rooftop landing pad for helicopters opened. In addition to excellent connections to buses and subways, the complex now boasted direct transportation to Kennedy International Airport. After three years, however, this shuttle service stopped operating. Five months after it had reopened, on January 1, 1977, a fatal accident caused the helipad to close permanently.

above: Grand Central Terminal
left: MetLife Building in its urban context

A work of art made from brass wire: *Flight*

In 1981, MetLife purchased the building for $400 million. When the air-line went bankrupt in 1991, the large Pan Am logo was replaced by that of MetLife. In the summer of 2005, the building was sold to the real estate firm Tishman Speyer Properties for $1.72 billion, at the time a record price for an office building. This acquisition allowed the real estate company, founded in 1978, to increase its holdings of office and residential space to more than 65 million square feet. The total value of their real estate assets—among them the Chrysler Building (page 88), the Rockefeller Center (page 150), and the Frankfurt Messeturm (Fair Tower)—is more than $20 billion. Despite the sale of the MetLife Building, the insurance company retains its office floors, and holds the right to display its logo on the building.

Adjacent to the MetLife Building on its south side is Grand Central Termi-nal, completed in 1913. This masterwork of Beaux-Arts classicism, with one of New York's most splendid interiors, is captivating primarily by virtue of its main concourse, which measures more than 360 feet in length and 120 feet in width. In 1998, in the course of extensive renovations, the cupola was restored, among other areas. Its vaulted ceiling decoration is of a firmament featuring astrological signs and more than 2,500 individual stars. The facade of the monumental exterior features enormous arched openings on all sides, each flanked by powerful columns. Set above the roof edge on the 42nd Street entrance is a large clock face decorated with figures representing mythologi-cal gods.

The vigorous public criticism of the Pan Am Building directed at its over-bearing presence in relation to Grand Central Terminal was one of many mo-tives for the establishment in the mid-1960s of New York City's Landmarks Preservation Commission. Consequently, the completion of this office com-plex indirectly resulted in greater attention being paid to the protection and preservation of historically important buildings.

HELMSLEY BUILDING

(ALSO KNOWN AS 230 PARK AVENUE; FORMERLY NEW YORK CENTRAL BUILDING)

ADDRESS	STORIES	COMPLETION	HEIGHT	ARCHITECT
230 Park Avenue	34	1928	565 feet	Warren & Wetmore

The Helmsley Building is among the most vivid examples of a skyscraper that forms part of a coherent urban fabric. It is adapted almost perfectly to its unique site, north of Grand Central Terminal, and it allows the city to literally traverse it. As the New York Central Building, it originally served as the headquarters of the New York Railroad Company. The short Vanderbilt Avenue on its west side was named in honor of Cornelius Vanderbilt, founder of the railway company. At the time, the building's placement directly above Park Avenue meant that it blocked views along the heavily trafficked north-south axis. Nonetheless, it harmonized with the adjacent development in a way utterly lacking in the Pan Am Building (page 114), erected 30 years later. In the 1960s, when the area around Grand Central Terminal experienced intensified development, the Helmsley Building—once the district's preeminent structure—would find itself languishing in the shadow of the new International Style office towers. Yet because of its exceptional location and extraordinary design, it remains to this day a striking landmark on the New York skyline.

In 1913, the replacement of steam locomotives by electric trains led to the reconstruction of Grand Central Terminal. The nation's first fully electrified train station was built along a subterranean route that extended for 16 blocks. Due to these underground train lines, the buildings erected above have an unusual foundation. The most spectacular element of this particular city block is the Helmsley Building with its base, clad in pale limestone. It was given a pair of arched portals through which the street traffic of Park Avenue moves in both directions. Resting on the cornice above the entrance on the north side is a decorated clock flanked by gilded sculptures of the mythological gods Mercury and Ceres. Mercury, the Messenger of the Gods, symbolizes transportation, while Ceres, the goddess of agriculture, is an emblem of the grain that is transported by railway.

Rising above the base to a height of 28 stories is the shaft of the Helmsley Building. Set above it on each side is a three-story-high colonnade, each with eight columns. Beginning two stories above is the copper roof, distinguished by its gold decorations and oval windows. The now shimmering green roof is pyramidal in form, and culminates in a gilded neoclassical cupola. In the evening, both upper sections of the building are brightly lit, giving them a far stronger impact than they have during the daytime. Flanking the central tower on the east and west sides are two 15-story units containing the larger portion of the 1.3 million square feet of gross floor area. The lobby is decorated with gleaming travertine floors, marble walls, and opulent chandeliers.

At the time of its completion, the Helmsley Building—with its classic, expressive forms—did not correspond to the emergent Art Deco zeitgeist. It was all the more capable, then, of responding to the monumental style of the adjacent Grand Central Terminal. In 1987, it was granted landmark status.

above: Mercury and Ceres flank the clock face above the north entrance
left: Total view from the north

UNION CARBIDE BUILDING

(NOW JP MORGAN CHASE WORLD HEADQUARTERS)

ADDRESS	STORIES	COMPLETION	HEIGHT	ARCHITECT
270 PARK AVENUE	52	1960	707 FEET	GORDON BUNSHAFT OF SKIDMORE, OWINGS & MERRILL

Total view from the north east

When the Union Carbide Building was built in 1960, it was New York City's tallest skyscraper in nearly 30 years. At that time, with a gross floor area of more than 1.9 million square feet, it was one of the largest office buildings in the world. At the same time, it was one of the last high-rises to be subject to the New York Zoning Resolution of 1916. The complex extends the length of an entire city block on the northern end of Vanderbilt Avenue, and consists of two contrasting structures: a 52-story office tower that is set back several yards from the sidewalks of Park Avenue, and a 13-story annex adjoining the tower on its western side. This arrangement takes maximum advantage of the building codes. The presence of the rail system of Grand Central Terminal running beneath the building prevents the foundation from being sunk to a sufficient depth. The supporting columns are therefore set on the preexisting load-bearing system of the subway and underground railway lines.

At the time, the structural system used by Gordon Bunshaft for the Union Carbide Building represented an exemplary solution to the problems of high-rise load distribution, insulation, and weatherproofing, as well as to the problem of wind-force resistance. Equally skillful are the installations for lighting and ventilation, which, together with the loudspeaker system, are found in the ceiling interspaces. For optimal air exchange, the ceilings themselves were perforated. Milk-colored plastic panels mounted at the ceilings provide the individual sources of light and produce a uniform illumination, one that makes an extraordinary impression, particularly in the evening hours.

Escalators carry visitors from the street level entrance area to the lobby on the first upper floor. This space, designed by Natalie de Blois, has a grand ceiling height of 26 feet. Although these dimensions make the space ideal for a variety of exhibitions, it usually goes unnoticed by the public because of its remove from the street. Rising from this level are elevators, which are prevented by subway tracks from reaching the ground floor. Standing at the southeastern section of the site, at the intersection of Park Avenue and 47th Street, is J. Seward Johnson's bronze sculpture *Taxi*, installed in 1983, which depicts a businessman hailing a cab.

Because of its functional structure, the Union Carbide Building is often referred to as the "Seagram Building by Skidmore, Owings & Merrill." In fact, it lacks both the technical perfection and the widespread acceptance of its celebrated predecessor (page 124). After the Union Carbide chemical corporation sold its building in the 1980s, it changed hands a number of times. Today, it is the headquarters of JP Morgan Chase & Co., created in 2000 following the takeover of JP Morgan Bank by Chase Manhattan Bank.

Extension of the building on the western side

WALDORF= ASTORIA HOTEL

ADDRESS	STORIES	COMPLETION	HEIGHT	ARCHITECT
301 Park Avenue	47	1931	625 feet	Schultze & Weaver

On October 25, 1929, one day after the great stock market crash on Wall Street, a contract was signed for the construction of the Waldorf=Astoria Hotel. This new grand hotel replaced an older structure bearing the same name, which had been demolished in the late 1920s to make way for the Empire State Building (page 74). When the Waldorf=Astoria Hotel went into operation in 1931 after just two years of construction, its 2,200 rooms made it the largest hotel in the world. The design of the exterior, with its pair of Art-Deco-style towers and solid masonry work, looks to the architecture of the late 1920s rather than the more clear structures of the new decade.

The hotel's massive base takes up an entire urban block between Park and Lexington Avenues. Rising above it between the 21st and 47th stories is an exclusive section known as the "Waldorf Towers," which, in addition to hotel rooms, contains private apartments, with an entrance on 50th Street. The best-known unit is the presidential suite on the 35th floor, the traditional overnight accommodations for U.S. presidents during stays in New York City. The upper terminus of the building consists of a pair of towers covered by rounded copper roofs.

Dominating the lower stories is a profusion of ballrooms, shops, restaurants, and nightclubs. When the hotel opened, this arrangement was a novelty, resembling an independent city under a single roof. The plush windowless lobby recalls the style of many European luxury hotels, with its regal wall and floor coverings, valuable statues and furniture, ornate chandeliers, and black granite columns. Additional points of interest in the entrance area include Louis Rigal's Mosaic *The Wheel of Life* and a 10-foot-high clock whose octagonal pedestal features the portraits of seven American presidents and an image of Queen Victoria. Its chimes, which ring every quarter hour, imitate those of London's Westminster Cathedral. Located at the east entrance on Lexington Avenue is the "Bull and Bear" steakhouse and bar, famous for its outstanding steaks. Those preferring lighter fare can order the famous Waldorf salad, created by the hotel's first head chef, Oskar Tschirky.

Like many other high-rises on Park Avenue, the Waldorf=Astoria Hotel was erected directly above the railway system leading to Grand Central Terminal. In the early years, it had its own holding track, accessible to hotel guests directly via elevator. The time-honored "Starlight Roof" was the meeting point of America's high society at the time. In the 1930s and 1940s, radio broadcasts were sent regularly from the roof of the 20-story Park Avenue wing. While the glamour of former times appears somewhat faded today, the Waldorf=Astoria Hotel remains one of the best-known, largest, and most elegant hotels in the city. Beginning in 2003, the hotel's name has been written with an equal sign, intended to recall the traditional manner of writing the names of both of the old hotels ("The Waldorf" and "The Astoria") on 34th Street.

above: Towers of the Waldorf=Astoria Hotel
center: Entrance on Park Avenue
below: Clock in the hotel lobby

SEAGRAM BUILDING

ADDRESS	STORIES	COMPLETION	HEIGHT	ARCHITECT
375 Park Avenue	38	1958	515 feet	Ludwig Mies van der Rohe, Philip Johnson

The consummate expression of the ideals of the International Style skyscraper is the Seagram Building. It embodies the essence of modernist architecture with a purity and elegance never achieved before or after its construction. Who would be better suited to realize Mies van der Rohe's principles of order, logic and clarity than Mies van der Rohe himself. To mark the 100th anniversary of the Seagram Company, the firm's CEO, Samuel Bronfman, wanted to build a new office building on Park Avenue. Although originally the architectural firm of Pereira & Luckman was intended for the job, Bronfman's daughter, the young architect Phyllis Lambert, persuaded her father that the new headquarters of the spirits and beverage company should be the work of a prestigious architect with international standing. Together with Philip Johnson, she was able to recruit Mies van der Rohe for the project. The Seagram Building was his first corporate high-rise, and would remain Mies's sole realized project in New York City.

Everything about the Seagram Building followed a rigorously thought-through and seamless organization. The constructive clarity of this office tower excludes the possibility of ornamentation and facade art. The plan is based on a uniform grid of vertical struts, arranged at intervals of 28 feet. These subdivide the facade into five units on its long sides and three on the short ones. The exposed structure contemplated by Mies van der Rohe, however, violated U.S. building codes, which stipulated that load-bearing steel elements had to be encased in a fireproof material. He solved this problem by sheathing the steel skeleton in concrete, which was in turn enclosed in a bronze-colored layer of steel. Another novel element for the time was the use of floor-to-ceiling bronze-tinted windows. In conjunction with the continuously arranged railing elements, they endow the Seagram Building with a uniform, vertical facade profile.

The rear portion of the site is occupied almost entirely by an ancillary building in the form of an inverted "T." Rarely visible from Park Avenue, this structure augments the usable floor space of the Seagram Building by more than one third. Located on the 52nd Street side is the entrance to the exclusive "Four Seasons" restaurant, intentionally placed at the back in order to maintain the building's overall uniform appearance. Philip Johnson was responsible for the structure's landscaped design.

above: Seagram Building in the evening hours
below: Ludwig Mies van der Rohe (1886–1969)

Underlying the design of the Seagram Building is an unmistakable contradiction: with its uniform surface structure and distinctive proportions, it embodies mechanical mass production. Yet at the same time, its interiors are characterized by individualized, hand-fashioned décor, and consummate detailing. The interior design was largely the work of Philip Johnson, who would later occupy a top-floor office. Like Mies van der Rohe, he was convinced that even the smallest details should contribute to the building's unified appearance. Among these are the lettering on the mailboxes and the specially designed door handles and bathroom fixtures. Even the window blinds can be opened and closed to three precisely defined intervals. The occasionally unrestrained choice of lavish materials for both interior and exterior areas was responsible for the exceptionally high costs—more than $36 million—for a skyscraper of these dimensions. In terms of square footage, the Seagram Building was the most expensive office high-rise in the world at the time of its completion.

A great achievement of the Seagram Building lies in its wholly new level of integration of a high-rise into an urban context. The office tower occupies only the rear half of a site measuring 200 x 300 feet. By locating the structure back 100 feet from the sidewalks of Park Avenue, Mies broke the uniform building line of the street-wall in a refreshing manner. The resulting public plaza is elevated on three steps, and hence removed from street traffic like a podium. Set at the sides are symmetrically arranged pools with fountains, as well as small landscaped areas. Borders of green Italian marble form seating areas that are used frequently by passersby.

Mies van der Rohe conceived of the public plaza in front of the building as a gift to New York's inhabitants. Designed to function as a kind of tranquil island within a metropolitan jungle, it has been taken up in this spirit by pedestrians. New York's city officials were so impressed with this arrangement of skyscraper and plaza that three years later the 1916 New York Zoning Resolution was revised. Among other changes, the new regulations contained a bonus system according to which new construction projects that included public space were permitted an increase in gross square footage by up to 20 percent. This provision spelled the end of the setback skyscraper whose lower stories often occupied the entire site. The ensuing years saw the erection of many build-ings in Manhattan that were fronted by plazas. Most of these surfaces, however, have deteriorated into uninviting, anonymous places.

With its clarity and attention to detail, the Seagram Building was regarded at the time of its construction as a model for a new high-rise architecture. Mies van der Rohe designed the structure as a freestanding, isolated monument. In contrast to earlier stylistic eras, however, its form offered few possibilities for variation. Numerous imitators felt justified in throwing up banal glass containers lacking any unified order or passion for detail. Most of these large office towers do the Seagram Building a disservice. Today, although celebrated as one of the great artworks of its time, it must deflect the charge that it set a negative pattern for the subsequent generation. For its unquestionably enormous contribution to the development of high-rise construction, the Seagram Building has received numerous distinctions from a variety of organizations. A good 30 years after its completion, it was granted landmark status by New York City's Landmarks Preservation Commission. In the early 21st century, RFR Realty purchased the building for $380 million dollars. Shortly before, this real estate company had acquired Lever House (page 128), which faces the Seagram Building at an angle, becoming the owner of perhaps the two most important International Style office buildings.

right: Uniform facade on Park Avenue
below: Model for a generation of skyscrapers:
The plaza in front of the Seagram Building

LEVER HOUSE

ADDRESS	STORIES	COMPLETION	HEIGHT	ARCHITECT
390 Park Avenue	21	1952	302 feet	Gordon Bunshaft of Skidmore, Owings & Merrill

Lever House is one of the outstanding architectural monuments of classic modernism. With its simple geometric forms, it signaled the transition in the early 1950s from European avant-gardism to commercial building in America. A new design element in the high-rise construction of the time was the configuration of space and light generated by the visual separation of the horizontal base from the vertical shaft of the office tower. Gordon Bunshaft, principal designer in the architectural firm of Skidmore, Owings & Merrill, combined earlier designs by Le Corbusier and Mies van der Rohe into a single, highly unified work. The radical opening of the building line not only represented an entirely new standard in high-rise construction but would also come to decisively affect building codes developed some 10 years later.

The podium-style base is dependent on Le Corbusier's piloti system, with the main body of the building elevated above ground level on supporting pillars. Rising above this base on the northern edge of the site is a 19-story high-rise slab. It is rotated 90 degrees from Park Avenue to form a right angle and it covers exactly 25 percent of the site. An additional novelty is the glass facade that is suspended from the steel skeleton, an idea that would revolutionize high-rise building in the following years. In contrast to the United Nations Secretariat Building (page 94), completed only shortly before, whose short sides are still clad in marble, Lever House displays a unified glass curtain wall on all four sides. This complete renunciation of masonry cladding generates a unique effect of lightness and openness. Although this glazing in fact represents a modernist version of ornamentalism, the structure does succeed in evoking the impression that it consists entirely of glass.

The horizontal facade profile is formed of green-tinted windowpanes sectioned off by turquoise railing elements made of opaque glass. The contrasting characteristics of these materials are especially noticeable at dusk, when the illuminated office levels wrap around the building like bands of light. Because of the full climatization system, the windows couldn't be opened. This also protected the offices from dirt off the street. Since the outer surfaces of the windows of Lever House couldn't be cleaned from the inside, a new cleaning technique had to be devised. Window cleaners were lowered on gondolas from tracks mounted on the roof frame. Today, this

above: Lever House in the evening
right: Roof installation for window washing

technique—which also has the advantage that employees experience minimal disturbance during cleaning—is the general standard for high-rise buildings.

In the 1970s, serious consideration was given to demolishing the office tower. Its gross floor area of 280,000 square feet was seen as too small for this prominent location, under-utilizing it (the building's use of the site corresponded only to an eight-story building). Protests later led to the abandonment of these plans. In order to preempt subsequent considerations of this kind, the New York City Landmarks Preservation Commission gave the building protected status exactly 30 years after its erection (the earliest allowable for landmark status). The garden plaza and the adjacent lobby exhibits several works of art by artists such as Isamu Noguchi and Damien Hirst.

RITZ TOWER

(ALSO KNOWN AS THE RITZ HOTEL TOWER)

ADDRESS	STORIES	COMPLETION	HEIGHT	ARCHITECT
465 PARK AVENUE	41	1926	541 FEET	EMERY ROTH, THOMAS HASTINGS

The Ritz Tower, completed in 1926, is the world's first residential skyscraper. With a height of 541 feet, it once dominated northeastern midtown Manhattan. Until its construction, the majority of New York City's multifamily residential buildings featured compact ground plans, and none were taller than 200 feet. Their uniform height was a consequence of New York's strict laws governing residential development. While commercial office towers were subject solely to restrictions concerning their configuration of mass, residential buildings had to conform to height limitations. A clever strategy allowed the Ritz Tower to evade these provisions: managed by the Ritz Carlton Hotel Company, the building was designated an "apartment hotel." Since hotels did not fall under the category of residences, the 41-story structure was able to obtain a construction permit.

Emery Roth and Thomas Hastings designed the lower third of the Ritz Tower to resemble the palatial apartment buildings lining Park Avenue. The lowest three stories, clad in rusticated limestone paneling, are decorated with Italian Renaissance motifs. On the ground floor along with smaller shops was an elegantly decorated hotel-style restaurant. Opening several years later and operating for a number of years was the French restaurant "Le Pavillon," among the city's finest and most prominent culinary establishments. Today the lowest stories are home to a bookstore. Rising above the building's 19-story base is a slender tower that decreases telescopically in size as it approaches the apex. The capital is formed by a pyramidal, flattened copper roof at whose center an obelisk rises.

From the very beginning, the apartments in the Ritz Tower were among the city's most elegant and luxurious. Accordingly, they attracted a number of prominent residents, among them movie stars such as Greta Garbo and Deborah Kerr, as well as newspaper mogul William Randolph Hearst, who would later own the building. In addition to the upper-story apartments, which once featured unobstructed views extending to distances of 25 miles, apartments featuring terraces were especially coveted. The small roof gardens were formed by the setbacks of the tower, and were a novelty in their day. The showpiece is an apartment occupying the entire 18th and 19th stories, whose 23-foot ceilings are double the heights of the other units. A lavish range of services is available to all residents, including the comforts of a central kitchen.

above: Capital of the Ritz Tower
below: Ritz Tower with neighboring buildings

The Ritz Tower occupies a prominent position in architectural history, having contributed substantially to the realization of the vertical city. In this respect, it corresponds to a futuristic vision published in the early 20th century by Moses King under the title *King's Dream of New York*. King envisioned a city built in the skies, one whose apartment buildings, places of work, and transportation systems were all suspended at high altitudes. In the late 1920s, New York's residential building codes were relaxed in response to new demands. Although the Ritz relinquished much of its prominence in the subsequent decades, as the first residential skyscraper, it nonetheless played a special role in the developmental history of high-rise construction. In October 2002, the New York City Landmarks Preservation Commission acknowledged this status by placing the building under its protection.

FOUR SEASONS HOTEL

ADDRESS	STORIES	COMPLETION	HEIGHT	ARCHITECT
57 EAST 57TH STREET	52	1993	682 FEET	I. M. PEI & PARTNERS, FRANK WILLIAMS ASSOCIATES

In the early 1990s, the Four Seasons Hotel was erected on 57th Street on an empty site that was surrounded by earlier skyscrapers. The 52-story luxury hotel is the flagship of the hotel chain bearing the same name, and with a height of 682 feet, it is still currently the tallest hotel building in New York City. Well integrated into its urban context, the exterior incorporates the most salient characteristics of neighboring high-rises. Principal among these are its vertical window bays and stepped pedestal, above which rises a slender tower.

The design for this $400-million project came from the pen of Chinese-American architect Ieoh Ming (I.M.) Pei. For the Four Seasons Hotel, he selected a cream-colored limestone facade that features minimal but well-chosen details. Among these is the circular opening set above the 57th Street entrance. Set on the individual setbacks are small iron lanterns that illuminate the hotel with extraordinary splendor after sunset. The monumental base gives way to a tower whose edges have been sliced away and is itself terminated by a stepped crown. Its floor-to-ceiling window bays and project-

ing balconies, which engage in a dialogue with those of the adjacent Fuller Building (page 133) to the west, acquired their current design with the remodeled pinnacle of the building in 2003.

The hotel lobby derives its character from its octagonal columns, patterned flooring, and Art Deco lamps. This space, 30 feet in height, is illuminated unobtrusively by ceiling lamps mounted beneath a grid of onyx. The 310 guest rooms and 60 suites offered by the hotel complex are all decorated tastefully with expensive furnishings. With an average size of 600 square feet, the rooms are among New York's largest and most expensive. The undisputed prize among these is the 4,300-square-foot "Ty Warner Penthouse" on the 52nd floor. With a price tag of $30,000 dollars per night, it is the world's most expensive overnight accommodations. The two 1,500-square-foot presidential suites just below in the 51st floor offer comparable luxury for only half the price.

above: Hotel lobby
left: Total view from 57th Street
right: View from the north-west

FULLER BUILDING

ADDRESS	STORIES	COMPLETION	HEIGHT	ARCHITECT
41 East 57th Street	40	1929	492 feet	Walker & Gillette

Capital of the Fuller Building

Founded in 1882, the George A. Fuller Construction Company was already by the end of the 19th century among the leading American building firms. From the very beginning, it implemented the latest developments in high-rise construction, earning acclaim in particular in Chicago with such signature buildings as the Monadnock Building, the Rookery, and the Tacoma Building. Its best-known project by far was New York City's Flatiron Building (page 66), which was also its headquarters. In the late 1920s, after a decade of successful expansion, the company's directors decided to erect a new headquarters on 57th Street.

The Fuller Building is a typical Art Deco skyscraper with a slender and well-proportioned form. Most of its office space is located in the building's 18-story pedestal. The lower six levels of this section are characterized by a showcase window front whose panes are framed in black granite. The expansive glazed surfaces ensure that the stores occupying these levels receive sufficient daylight. Above the 10th story, this pedestal is tapered by means of numerous setbacks, and culminates in a tower that is square in plan. The building's surface design is relatively simple, and almost completely devoid of ornamentation. In contrast, the stepped capital reflects the spirit of Art Deco. Reminiscent of an Aztec temple, this form is embellished with triangles, zigzag patterns, and sun motifs on black-and-white terra-cotta.

The three-story-high entrance on 57th Street consists of two flattened pillars, an alternative to the more common classical columns. Above the building's name, these culminate in an elaborate bas-relief containing a clock face flanked by a pair of construction workers depicted before an abstract skyline. In contrast to the largely simple facade design, the lobby area is luxuriantly embellished with decorative elements. In addition to opulent lighting, there are the bronze panels in the elevators and round mosaics with elaborately rendered shadow effects set in the flooring. These depict some of the famous buildings constructed by the company.

Around 1930, an increasing number of art galleries began to replace the row of stores on the lower floors. Today, this section of 57th Street is still characterized by its numerous antiques dealers and art galleries, whose high prices reflect the neighborhood's rents.

View from street level

IBM BUILDING
(NOW 590 MADISON AVENUE)

ADDRESS	STORIES	COMPLETION	HEIGHT	ARCHITECT
590 MADISON AVENUE	43	1983	603 FEET	EDWARD LARRABEE BARNES ASSOCIATES

With its elongated prismatic form, the IBM Building offers a marked enhancement of New York's high-rise cityscape. Depending on the vantage point, the building's sculptural quality provides for vastly differing impressions of its overall shape. At the time of its construction, the building's pentagonal plan was a departure from the square and rectangular structures of the International Style. The smooth, uniform surfaces of its facades are covered in dark green polished granite and green-tinted windowpanes. While its horizontal articulation and flat roof have their roots in modernist architecture, the expressive form of the IBM Building belongs to postmodernism. This is especially evident in the use of granite as a facade material, an example of its manifest break with the style of the preceding 30 years. Its polished surface gives it a smoother look than most high-rises, with their stone claddings; at the same time, it is more evolved than the contemporary glass tower.

The lobby area at the northeast of the building is sliced open diagonally, opening up the field of vision at street level. As a result of this interruption, the remaining levels cantilever out into the intersection of Madison Avenue and 57th Street. The double-height lobby originally opened onto the IBM Gallery of Arts and Sciences on the north side. This space was intended as a gesture toward the numerous art galleries lining 57th Street. Following the relocation of the computer technology company in 1994, it was replaced by a public gallery. A red-steel sculpture by Alexander Calder stands in the main entrance and the plaza to the southeast is home to an environmental artwork by Michael Heizer, *Levitated Mass,* that features a large block of granite at the center of a flat stainless-steel fountain of rushing water.

At the southwestern section of the site, the office building is joined by the four-story-high skylit atrium. This landscape design is an encouraging instance of a skyscraper whose urban planning obligations do not interfere with its success as a work of architecture. The atrium, resembling a greenhouse, forms the eastern portion of a covered pedestrian walkway that connects to Trump Tower (page 142), which adjoins the building to the west. The interior is almost hermetically sealed off from the street noise of Madison Avenue, allowing visitors to forget that they are actually in the middle of hectic Manhattan. Its 11,000 square feet feature a large number of bamboo trees, a variety of artworks, and a generous selection of seating areas.

Together with the AT&T Building (page 136), adjacent on the south, and the Trump Tower adjacent on the west, the office tower known today as 590 Madison Avenue forms a trio of skyscrapers, all erected within a year of one another and within close range. While these three buildings are entirely different in their designs, all belong to the postmodern generation of high-rises. Nowhere else in the world are the diverse tendencies of this stylistic era displayed with comparable clarity and in such close proximity.

above: IBM Building with the Trump Tower (left) and the AT&T Building (right)
left: Skylit atrium of the IBM Building

AT&T BUILDING
(NOW SONY BUILDING)

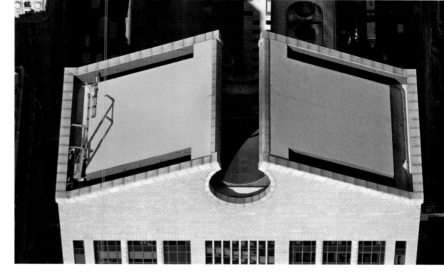

ADDRESS	STORIES	COMPLETION	HEIGHT	ARCHITECT
550 MADISON AVENUE	37	1984	647 FEET	JOHNSON & BURGEE

Virtually no other construction endeavor in New York before or after the AT&T Building, completed in 1984, has unleashed such intense public debate. The first great monument of postmodernism, it conclusively ended the protracted transition from late modernism to postmodernism. From the perspective of the early 1980s, an oppressive banality had prevailed in high-rise construction for more than three decades. With a few notable exceptions, all of these skyscrapers were firmly modeled on the International Style. By the late 1970s, there was an increasing desire for a return to the classical forms and the crown-style roofs of the Art Deco age. With his daring designs, it was Philip Johnson—of all people—who filled a broad public with enthusiasm for the new architectural style. The American architect, who was a close associate of Mies van der Rohe and who had once numbered among the great supporters of architectural modernism, now turned with equal resoluteness away from his former allegiances. With the AT&T Building, Johnson once against demonstrated his certainty of touch in recognizing the prevailing zeitgeist and in translating it into tangible form. While postmodernist buildings were never as loaded with ornamentation as those of the 1920s, functionality no longer occupied the foreground as the sole valid criterion.

The design for the AT&T Building was so sensational that in 1978 it was featured on the cover of Time magazine. At first glance, it evokes the tripartite building division advocated by Louis Sullivan. Its special achievement, however, lies in the way in which all three sections, despite being completely dissimilar, are nonetheless skillfully joined into a genuine unity. At the center of its frontage, oriented toward Madison Avenue, the base of the building features a 72-foot high round arched portal flanked by massive supporting elements. Toward the rear is a large atrium spanned by a glass arch. Set above the lower section of the building is a shaft that is relatively conventional in design; its facade is clad in unpolished pink granite. In contrast to many contemporary high-rises, Johnson's building makes no attempt to seize attention by means of a striking ground plan. The basic footprint is instead a standard rectangle. At the time, the capital constituted a radical departure from everything known up to that point. Its gable is "pierced" by a rounded opening 36 feet in diameter, giving the building the appearance of a Chippendale highboy.

The lower lobby, which features gilded cross vaulting in Romanesque style, has an impressive height of 65 feet. Only above this point does the office building begin, its floors stacked uniformly on top of one another. The elevation of the office levels, however, was not the result of design considerations, but instead conformed to the requirements of New York's zoning regulations intended to preserve the original character of Madison Avenue as a shopping street. Other requirements included the provision of public space, a demand satisfied by the arcades at Madison Avenue and the atrium.

The unusual form of the skyscraper attracted widespread critical attention. Many admired the building as an artistic masterstroke. Proponents of modernism, however, dismissed it as an object that merely strived for effect. In an allusion to the business of its client, it was ridiculed as resembling an oversized telephone cradle. Others simply referred to the building as the "Chippendale skyscraper."

above: Capital in "Chippendale-Design," seen from above
below: Atrium on the west side of the AT&T Building

left: Total view taken from the street
right: The AT&T Building in its urban
context

In the early 1990s the AT&T Corporation relocated from its main headquarters. Its new occu-
pant, the Sony Corporation, initiated a substantial
redesign of the pedestal section. The open arcades
were converted into closed units, which since then
have been given over to stores. The atrium on the
west side adjoins the Sony Wonder Technology
Lab, an interactive exhibition space for the latest
models and technologies of the electronics company.

The AT&T Building not only set the standard
for a new stylistic direction in high-rise building
but it also answered the question, what is postmodernist architecture. The building's overriding
significance, however, lies mainly in the influence
it exercised on architects, who were inspired to
undertake the final leap from modernism to postmodernism. With this design, Philip Johnson—who
by the late 1960s had conceded that America's
downtowns had grown uglier in the preceding
50 years—contributed decisively to the resurrec-
tion of the architectural visual interest that has
taken place over the past 30 years.

PHILIP JOHNSON—A PATHBREAKING 20ᵀᴴ-CENTURY ARCHITECT

Philip Cortelyou Johnson, born on July 8, 1906, in Cleveland, Ohio, influenced 20th-century building as perhaps no other architect. In 1932, as Director of Architecture and Design for New York's Museum of Modern Art, he organized a ground-breaking exhibition on the International Style, which demonstrated unmistakably to a global public that only Bauhaus modernism, with its characteristic steel-and-glass cladding, was the way of the future and capable of putting an end to the stylistic confusion of the preceding three decades. With his Glass House, built in New Canaan, Connecticut, in 1949, this great advocate of the works of Ludwig Mies van der Rohe became the first to realize a residence clad entirely in glass. Just a few years later, he worked together with Mies on the design of the Seagram Building in New York, still regarded as the prototypical International Style office high-rise.

Philip Johnson's great talent lay in his ability to recognize new tendencies in architecture very early on. In the late 1960s, it was Johnson who saw that modernism, with its objective of pure functionality, had reached a dead end. Formerly one of the principal advocates and founders of the International Style, Johnson, in his late modernist and post-modernist designs of the 1970s and 1980s, is responsible to a large degree for the fact that today high-rise architecture is once again a fascinating mix of contrasting colors and forms.

In 1979, Philip Johnson was the first architect to receive the Pritzker Prize—the highest distinction bestowed on an architect. His perhaps best-known postmodernist design, the AT&T Building in New York, was produced in the early 1980s in collaboration with his longtime business partner John Bur-

Philip Johnson (1906–2005)

gee. This project represents a key building in a career that lasted nearly seven decades. In 1988, Johnson organized the exhibition "Deconstructivist Architecture" at New York's Museum of Modern Art, through which architects such as Frank Gehry, Daniel Libeskind, and Rem Koolhaas achieved their international breakthroughs. In the late 1990s, the world finally bid farewell to the doyen of American architecture, a man whose enormous influence not infrequently involved him in controversy. On January 25, 2005, Philip Johnson died at his Glass House in New Canaan, at the age of 98.

CHAPTER

FIFTH AVENUE AND ROCKEFELLER CENTER

Along with its many luxury stores, Fifth Avenue, between 42nd street and 59th Street, can also boast an impressive assembly of skyscrapers, representing a wide range of eras and styles, which has grown over the decades, and contrasts sharply with the high-rise architecture of the Avenue of the Americas. In the 1960s and 1970s, several compact large-capacity skyscrapers were created in this densely built-up corridor of International Style structures. The centerpiece of this district, in terms of city-planning and architectural history, is formed by Rockefeller Center. This project, created in the 1930s, is a leading example of the successful integration of the high-rise building into the urban fabric.

KEY

55	Trump Tower
56	General Motors Building
57	Sherry-Netherland Hotel
58	Solow Building
59	Museum Tower
60	Olympic Tower
61	Rockefeller Center/G.E. Building
62	CBS Building
63	Time-Life Building
64	XYZ Buildings
65	W. R. Grace Building
66	500 Fifth Avenue
67	Fred F. French Building

TRUMP TOWER

ADDRESS	STORIES	COMPLETION	HEIGHT	ARCHITECT
725 Fifth Avenue	58	1983	664 feet	Der Scutt, Swanke Hayden Connell & Partners

Trump Tower is among New York's best-known building projects of the 1980s. The developer and owner of the building, the property titan Donald Trump, deemed it essential that this project demonstrate both on the exterior and the interior the qualities of luxury and glamour associated with his name. The most striking element of the building is its sliced-off facade on Fifth Avenue and its stepped base. As darkness falls, spotlights illuminate the small trees planted on the stepped levels, creating a glittering world of reflections that bring nature and urban luxury into harmony. By day, the Fifth Avenue facade reflects the Crown Building standing opposite, creating an interesting contrast between the limestone-clad 1920s building and the modern mirrored tower of the 1980s.

Apart from its outstanding location and impressive outward appearance, it is chiefly the extravagant interior decoration of Trump Tower that contributes to its reputation as a temple of luxury. The main entrance on Fifth Avenue is formed by a brass-clad entrance portal, leading to an atrium well worth visiting for its varied stores, restaurants, and cafés. The walls and floor gleam with brass and orange-colored marble. At the back of the atrium—below a glass ceiling, which supplies the area with additional, natural light—a floodlit waterfall cascades down from a height of 65 feet. At the top level of the shopping arcade is a small observation deck. As with the entrance to the Skylit atrium of the IBM Building (page 134), here, too, the view of the sky is characterized by the extraordinary contours of the neighboring high-rise buildings.

The 20 floors above the shopping arcade serve as office space (Donald Trump's company occupies the 26th floor). The higher levels accommodate 266 luxury apartments for members of the international jet set and are reached by a separate entrance on 56th Street. All the residential units feature views in three directions. The open vista to the northwest is the most breathtaking, stretching from Central Park to the George Washington Bridge at the tip of Manhattan. The jewel of the living quarters is the three-story, 53-room penthouse apartment surrounded by a roof garden, which Donald Trump reserved for himself.

The mixed use of Trump Tower was a precondition of approval for the building project at its present size. As with Olympic Tower (page 149), which stands somewhat farther south, a few years earlier, advantage was taken of the special bonus program that applied to this section of Fifth Avenue. This provided that all new buildings contributing to the preservation of the original streetscape by means of retail or residential units be granted spatial concessions as a bonus. The acquisition of the air rights of the adjacent jewelers, Tiffany & Co., meant that the gross floor area of Trump Tower could be increased to more than 750,000 square feet. When it was completed in 1983 after a construction period of almost four years, the tower for a brief time could claim to be the tallest building in New York supported by a concrete frame.

above: View from the east
below: The atrium with waterfall

GENERAL MOTORS BUILDING

ADDRESS	STORIES	COMPLETION	HEIGHT	ARCHITECT
767 Fifth Avenue	50	1968	705 feet	Edward Durell Stone, Emery Roth & Sons

This premier site at the junction of Fifth Avenue and 59th Street was at one time the location of the venerable Savoy Plaza Hotel, which during the first half of the 20th century was considered one of the best addresses in New York. After the Savoy was demolished in the mid-1960s, the site became the location of the General Motors Building, a huge complex that would interrupt the once uniform character of the area. The 50-story office tower demonstrates a vain attempt by the architect, Edward Durell Stone, to move away from the modernist glass-and-steel box and hark back to the stone-clad skyscrapers of the prewar period. This former New York base for the major automotive company was at the same time the first important high-rise design by this renowned architect (also responsible for, among others, Radio City Hall and the Museum of Modern Art).

Including its two underground floors, the General Motors Building has a gross floor area of 1.8 million square feet, making it one of the typical large-scale office boxes of the 1960s, whose functional appearance seemed more important than its connection with its urban context. Its facade consists of a finely meshed network of marble-clad pillars. The interstitial spaces are formed by a series of windows in dark glass, slightly set back from the facade. By means of the slight protrusion of the central unit and the vertical structures, the architect attempted to create a differentiation from the skyscrapers of the preceding 15 years. Nevertheless, the result of his efforts is an intimidating and impersonal building, which can be distinguished only superficially from its contemporaries.

The original design actually provided for a base that would cover the entire site, topped by a huge high-rise structure. Later, Stone decided in favor of the present—and unquestionably better variation—with a plaza of some 21,000 square feet placed in front of the building. The positioning of the building to the west of the site ensures that the slab-shaped structure is set back from Fifth Avenue and thus does not restrict the view along this boulevard. In spite of its central location, the plaza was for a long time just one more example of abortive urban planning. The windswept site was likewise long avoided because of its anonymity. After Donald Trump and the insurance company Conseco acquired the General Motors Building in 1998 for a sum of $800 million, a new design was introduced for the plaza, including greenery, retail, and two fountains. In the summer of 2006 the plaza was again rebuilt. At its center now stands a 33-foot-tall glass cube, from which visitors can reach the underground Apple Store by means of an elevator or a glass spiral staircase.

Its exposed position and generous floor area make the General Motors Building one of the most expensive office buildings worldwide. In the summer of 2008 its sale to a consortium of investors for $2.9 billion marked a record price for a single skyscraper. During its early years, its vast entrance area showcased the latest automobiles produced by the General Motors Corporation. The large, well-known toy emporium FAO Schwarz occupies the southern wing, while the northern part currently is used by CBS as a television studio.

above: Glass cube above the Apple Store
left: Total view of the building from the west

SHERRY- NETHERLAND HOTEL

ADDRESS	STORIES	COMPLETION	HEIGHT	ARCHITECT
781 Fifth Avenue	38	1927	560 feet	Schultze & Weaver

Between Fifth Avenue and Columbus Circle, 59th Street marks the southern border of Central Park. Over the last 100 years, many of the city's finest and most luxurious hotels have settled in this area. A distinctive group of these hotels was constructed at the intersection of 59th Street and Fifth Avenue, the best known of these buildings being the New York Plaza. Considerably more striking, however, is the Sherry-Netherland Hotel to the northeast of the intersection. With its romantic silhouette, it has long been the dominant element in this neighborhood.

Although neoclassicism had already been condemned as an anachronism by architectural critics by the mid-1920s, the Baroque tower and Gothic spire of the Sherry-Netherland demonstrate that in 1927 neoclassical stylistic elements still exercised an influence on the design of New York's high-rise buildings. The lower half of the structure consists of a compact base that becomes slimmer between the 18th and 24th floors in several stages. Above this, a slender 14-story tower rises on the west side, closed off by an imposing finial. With its projecting bay windows, its Gothic waterspouts, and minaret-like spire, the top of the building is more reminiscent of a church tower than the capital of a skyscraper.

Like the Ritz Tower (page 130), built slightly earlier, the Sherry-Netherland Hotel was granted the designation of apartment hotel, meaning that restrictions on residential building in New York at that time could be circumvented. At a height of 560 feet, it was in 1927 the fourth-tallest building in the city, and at the same time the tallest residential building in the world. Today, 97 out of the 150 luxuriously designed accommodations are used as permanent residences and are individually decorated and furnished. Particularly desirable are those apartments above the 24th floor, which extend over an entire story. Their occupants, who include many show business greats, enjoy an unspoiled view of the green spaces of Central Park as well as of the street life of midtown Manhattan.

above: Facade decoration as seen from the street
right: Total view from 59th street

SOLOW BUILDING
(ALSO KNOWN AS 9 WEST 57TH STREET)

ADDRESS	STORIES	COMPLETION	HEIGHT	ARCHITECT
9 West 57th Street	50	1974	689 feet	Gordon Bunshaft of Skidmore, Owings & Merrill

As early as the mid-1960s, the architect Gordon Bunshaft had developed designs for a building whose wide base narrowed in a swooping curve to a slender high-rise slab. But it was not until 10 years later that he was able to translate his idea into reality with the construction of the Solow Building. With the constantly changing corner in the lower third of the structure, this 50-story office building brought a new standard to New York's high-rise architecture and represented an alternative to the earlier stepped skyscrapers. Above all, however, at the time of its completion the curved form marked an increasingly pronounced move away from the boxy shapes of the last two decades. Many critics even see in it a precursor of the postmodern buildings of the following decade.

The impressive facades on the broad north and south sides of the Solow Building consist of dark mirror glass, framed at their edges by white travertine. At the narrow east and west sides, the building is fronted by massive steel cross-strutting, a typical feature of the work of Skidmore, Owings & Merrill at that time. In spite of an attempt to create a less overbearing effect on its neighbors with its elegant, tapering outline and its set back position behind the building line, the Solow Building remains a powerful mid-block intruder into a streetscape populated by smaller, more modest structures. This effect is strengthened by the fact, that this structure, built on an empty lot in between two buildings, seems to compress the many smaller surrounding edifices. The juxtaposition of old and new structures exerts an interesting optical tension on the viewer, but at the expense of the lower buildings.

Since September 2000, the restaurant "Brasserie 8 1/2" has occupied the basement, accessible by way of a glassed entrance area on 57th Street. In front stands a red-steel sculpture by Ivan Chermayeff in the form of the numeral 9, a reference to the building's address. The larger plaza on the north side features a sculpture by Pablo Picasso of a mythic bull.

above: Total view from the north-east
left: Entrance on 57th Street

MUSEUM TOWER

ADDRESS	STORIES	COMPLETION	HEIGHT	ARCHITECT
11 WEST 53RD STREET	52	1984	588 FEET	CESAR PELLI & ASSOCIATES

New York's Museum of Modern Art was one of the first art collections dedicated exclusively to contemporary art. Beginning in 1929 as a small exhibition space only a few yards northeast of its current location, over the ensuing years this structure has transformed into one of the most important museums of art worldwide. In the 1970s, because of the large accumulation of exhibits, only a fraction of the objects of art could be displayed. For its 50th anniversary, the museum decided to undertake a large-scale expansion, which would almost double its exhibition space. The financing of the conversion was enabled by the sale of air rights for a new skyscraper to be created above the museum.

After a five-year phase of planning and building, Museum Tower was completed in 1984. The architect Cesar Pelli was responsible for the design of the residential skyscraper, which rises above a six-story atrium. At the time of its completion, this slender 588-foot tower was among the world's tallest and most luxurious purely residential buildings. Its 240 residential units range from small studio apartments to two-story penthouses. Even though the museum and the residential tower are two self-sufficient entities, they represent a unified composition.

The facade cladding of the Museum Tower in the form of a cascade-like curtain wall, consisting of opaque blue and gray glass is a notable feature. With its clear gridlike lines, the 52-story structure stands out from its surroundings—without looking abstract, it is a work of art in its own right. Some early critics, who were eager to give their opinion, even before the completion of the building, found the building not commensurate with the lofty artistic expression expected from a structure above such an important museum. Others found fault with the infill structure on the grounds that it destroyed the streetscape characterized by low brownstone buildings.

above: Capital of the Museum Tower
below: Total view of the building
from the east

OLYMPIC TOWER

ADDRESS	STORIES	COMPLETION	HEIGHT	ARCHITECT
645 Fifth Avenue	51	1976	620 feet	Skidmore, Owings & Merrill

In Olympic Tower, completed in 1976, retail stores, offices, and luxury apartments were for the first time combined in a New York high-rise building. The mixed-use complex is based on zoning regulations that were revised in 1971 especially for this section of Fifth Avenue to counter the proliferation of banks, airline ticketing offices, and similar businesses in the area during the 1950s and 1960s. New buildings that offered a mixed use were allowed to increase the floor space up to 20 percent. Olympic Tower, commissioned by the Greek shipping magnate Aristotle Onassis, was the first high-rise to make use of this special bonus. An architecture critic later commented derisively that here, instead of an anonymous office tower, an anonymous mixed-use building had been created.

The potential for varied use in Olympic Tower also had a direct influence on the building's supporting structure. While the office floors from the 2nd to the 21st story were supported by a steel framework, the residential units above them are framed in concrete. The 225 residential units on the upper 30 stories all have floor-to-ceiling windows and are reached from a separate entrance on 51st Street. One of the two-story penthouse apartments was at one time occupied by Adnan Khashoggi, a Saudi businessman and arms dealer known for his extravagant lifestyle, who among other features installed a swimming pool extending over two floors.

The reflectivity of the bronze-colored glass surface is most evident in the south-facing facade, where it mirrors St. Patrick's Cathedral, standing one block to the south. This creates a contrast rich in tension between old and new development. On account of its height of 620 feet, Olympic Tower gives the impression that the 339-foot-high cathedral is considerably smaller than it actually is. In the eastern part of the site, a landscaped gallery leads north to south through the building. In the basement of the gallery, the Onassis Cultural Center opened its doors in the fall of 2000.

above: Olympic Tower with St. Patrick's Cathedral in the foreground
right: Total view of the building from the south
left: Gallery with the attached Onassis Cultural Center

ROCKEFELLER CENTER / G.E. BUILDING

(FORMERLY RCA BUILDING)

ADDRESS	STORIES	COMPLETION	HEIGHT	ARCHITECT
30 ROCKEFELLER PLAZA	70	1933	850 FEET	ROCKEFELLER CENTER ASSOCIATES ARCHITECTS

Rockefeller Center, built between 1932 and 1940, represents one of the key points in the history of the high-rise. As the first large-scale, privately financed, mixed-use urban redevelopment project in the United States, it was at the same time the only major private project in New York undertaken between the Great Depression and World War II. The actual starting signal for its construction was given as early as 1927, when John D. Rockefeller Jr. rented a redevelopment area of about 15 acres between Fifth Avenue and the Avenue of the Americas. 13 years were to elapse between the start of planning, which involved among other things the demolition of 200 houses, and the final completion of the project. With a total expenditure of $125 million, it was at that date the most costly skyscraper project of all time. In the middle of the Depression, it made a positive statement and provided new employment for more than 4,000 people.

The architects were a committee made up of the firms of Reinhard & Hofmeister, Corbett, Harrison & McMurray, and Hood & Fouilhoux. The last-named, under the overall supervision of Raymond Hood, was responsible for significant parts of the realization. The complex comprised 14 buildings (later increased to 21) of varying height, which, with a lower-level plaza, promenades, retail stores, and theaters, formed a city-within-the-city. From the viewpoint of skyscraper design and contemporary high-rise planning, however, its most important feature was the fact that an arrangement of high-rises were here presented as a total composition, forming a unique symbiosis of architecture and urban organism. Raymond Hood, the noted architect who had placed his personal stamp so firmly on the project, was not able to witness its completion. He died in 1934, at the age of 53.

above: Central point of the complex: The G.E. Building
below: Radio City Music Hall on the Avenue of the Americas

While the concept of the Rockefeller Center was a purely commercial one, when considering its total aesthetics, its artistic components and the public use of the complex should also be of considerable importance. The basic idea of the project consisted in the question: why should people not be able to shop, eat, or relax in the building where they worked? In its architectural style, the Rockefeller Center combined past and contemporary trends, bringing into harmony the lavish urban planning neo-classicism of the Beaux Arts style, the ornamentation of Art Deco, and the clarity of Modernism. Today more than 200 retail outlets or service companies are housed in its spaces, and every day this complex, with its 14 million square feet of gross floor area, receives more than 250,000 visitors. In addition its estimated purchase value of 15 billion dollars makes the Rockefeller Center currently the most costly property worldwide.

The focus of the structural ensemble is formed by the 850-foot-high G.E. Building (in full, General Electric Building). In order to obtain planning permission for this high-rise of more than 2.1 million square feet of gross floor area, the center of the complex had

to be considered as one site. Its structure was to a great extent the work of Raymond Hood. The slab-shaped structure of reinforced concrete consists of a series of slender, cascading setbacks. On the north and south sides, the lower levels of the 70-story building extend to 330 feet. The narrower fronts on the east and west sides, conversely, are only 105 feet wide and taper by a further 33 feet on their way to the top. As a result the structure on the one hand gives the impression of a large, projecting wall, but on the other hand also that of a slim tower, appearing to soar endlessly into the sky.

The lobby of the G.E. Building is notable chiefly for its murals by the Spanish painter José Maria Sert. Another wall mural, *Man at the Crossroads*, by Diego Rivera, also created here, was removed by the client, before the opening of the building, because it included a portrait of Lenin. Like the supply lines, the elevator shafts with their 60 high-speed elevators are located at the center of the building. Their number, decreasing as higher one goes, corresponds with the stepped levels of the outer facade. The office units are arranged around this internal core, with the distance from the corridor wall to the windows amounting to a maximum of 27 feet throughout the building. Hood explained that this was the greatest possible distance to ensure adequate access to daylight as well as a sufficient supply of fresh air. Apart from the NBC Studios, where visitors can watch a television program being produced, it is particularly rewarding to ride up to the observation decks known as "Top of the Rock," reopened in the fall of 2005, on the 67th to 70th floors (open daily from 8:30 a.m. till midnight). From this vantage point—and from the Rainbow Room, the restaurant located on the 65th floor, superbly furnished in Art Deco style—visitors can enjoy one of the finest views of the urban skyline.

In 1985 the G.E. Building, popularly known as "The Slab" or "30 Rock," became a New York City landmark. The most famous photograph of the building was taken during its construction in September 1932, when the photographer Charles C. Ebbets recorded workers sitting on a steel girder during their lunch break. Titled *Lunchtime Atop a Skyscraper*, it sold in the millions. Among the first tenants of Rockefeller Center were radio and television companies such as RCA (Radio Corporation of America) and the RKO film company, which together built an entertainment complex called Radio City. Particular recognition should be given to Radio City Music Hall on the Avenue of the Americas, with its splendid Art Deco design. With

above left: Sculpture of Atlas in front of the International Building
above center: Relief *Wisdom and Knowledge* at the eastern entrance of the G.E. Building
above right: Sculpture of Prometheus by Paul Manship
below right: Ceiling fresco in the lobby of the G.E. Building
left: The courtyard in front of the G.E. Building

more than 6,000 seats and 1 million visitors a year, it is today still among the largest theaters in the world.

At the northeast of the complex, between 50th and 51st Street, is the International Building, completed in 1935. At a height of 512 feet, it was for more than two decades the second-highest building in Rockefeller Center. From the outside, with its uniformly arranged setbacks and vertically structured limestone facade, it looks like a miniature version of the G.E. Building. On its east side, facing Fifth Avenue, is a notable sculpture of Atlas by Lee Lawrie and René Chambellan.

The public space of Rockefeller Center is just as impressive as the building itself. From Fifth Avenue, a wide T-shaped mall leads into the heart of the center. It also frequently serves as backdrop for open-air art exhibitions. A few yards to the west, at the foot of the G.E. Building, is the so-called "Sunken Plaza." This lower-level area is used in winter as an ice-skating rink and in summer as a café. Surrounded by an ocean of flags, it includes a fountain on its west side, in front of which rises Paul Manship's gilded bronze statue of Prometheus. Between this area and the entrance to the G.E. Building, which features Lee Lawrie's relief *Wisdom and Knowledge*, runs Rockefeller Plaza, a small private street. Since 1931 a gigantic Christmas tree has been put up here every year in late fall. When its 27,000 electric lights are switched on, the Christmas season in New York has officially begun.

CBS BUILDING

ADDRESS	STORIES	COMPLETION	HEIGHT	ARCHITECT
51 West 52nd Street	38	1965	492 feet	Eero Saarinen

View from the south-west

The headquarters of the Columbia Broadcasting System (CBS), completed in 1965, was part of the large-scale redevelopment of the Avenue of the Americas, whose (mostly deteriorated) sites were acquired at relatively low prices in the early 1960s. The box-shaped office tower has a ground plan of 130 x 164 feet and rises, uninterrupted, to a height of nearly 500 feet. In its outward form, the CBS Building followed contemporary structures, but in one decisive respect it broke away from the design features dominant at the time: in contrast to the horizontally structured skyscrapers of the International Style, here the expression is unmistakably vertical in emphasis. This effect results mainly from the five-foot-wide parallel triangular struts running from the ground floor to the roof, made of reinforced concrete, which replace the more usual steel struts. The corridor between the outer support system and the inner core dispenses with supports, and allows the individual floor surfaces greater flexibility in terms of use and design.

The roughened anthracite-colored granite cladding of the struts and their massive appearance lend an elegantly melancholy abstraction to the building. In interplay with the railing bars their tight arrangement gives the slightly set back windows the appearance of small television screens. In addition, the sharp-edged pillars produce strong outlines of light and shade, which, observed from various angles, allow a variety of impressions of the structure. Thus the windows disappear from an acute angle behind the projecting strut supports, giving the surface the appearance of a windowless wall. The story above the lobby, like the 38th story, is reserved for mechanical installations. Each of these levels supplies half the building. The 16 elevators also are divided into two banks. Eight elevators travel from the first to the 21st story, while the other eight serve the upper stories.

The use of dark granite cladding was intended to distinguish the CBS Building from its neighbors and earned it the popular nickname of "Black Rock." The modernist tendency to differentiate from surrounding structures had already been successfully undertaken in the futuristic Seagram Building (page 124) and the no less significant Lever House (page 128). In contrast to these buildings, however, Saarinen's skyscraper has 38 uniform stories, without hidden extensions or a wide base. The office tower, set back by 26 feet on all sides from the pavement, is fronted on the Avenue of the Americas by a sunken plaza, which forms a boundary from the frequently overcrowded sidewalks.

Although the CBS Building is a freestanding structure, its sculptural appearance scarcely comes into its own because of the density of the streetwall. While here the new geometric forms determined only the facade details, within a few years the general outline of skyscrapers was to take on new forms as well. Eero Saarinen did not live to experience the great recognition of his design, which was to exert a decisive influence on the later generation of high-rise buildings. The Finnish architect, whose designs for furniture (such as the "Tulip Chair") and airport buildings (including the TWA Terminal at Kennedy Airport in New York and Dulles Airport in Washington, D.C.) were awarded top design prizes, died in 1961 at the age of 51, long before the completion of the CBS Building.

TIME-LIFE BUILDING

ADDRESS	STORIES	COMPLETION	HEIGHT	ARCHITECT
1271 Avenue of the Americas	48	1958	587 feet	Harrison, Abramovitz & Harris

Between 42nd and 55th Street, office towers stand in dense rows along the Avenue of the Americas. Up to the mid-1950s, when the New York building authorities decided to give a new face to the somewhat banal district between Fifth Avenue and Broadway, this corridor still consisted of comparatively low-level buildings. For the envisioned new development, the authorities attempted to attract potential clients by means of low sales prices for the sites. The central and largest project was the western extension of Rockefeller Center between 47th and 51st Street. A start on this project was made in 1958 by the Time-Life Building. Apart from accommodating the needs of the publishing company, the design was also intended to create a visual connection with the existing buildings of Rockefeller Center (page 150). The commission was given to the office of Harrison, Abramovitz & Harris, whose architect Wallace K. Harrison had already worked on the design of Rockefeller Center some 30 years earlier. The functionalist Time-Life Building avoids stylistic details. In the years that followed, its boxy shape represented the most frequently imitated prototype for skyscrapers in midtown Manhattan.

above: *Cube Curved* by William Crovello
below: Plaza on the Avenue of the Americas

In contrast to the facade cladding of the older structures in Rockefeller Center, the Time-Life Building was given a curtain wall in contemporary style, of greenish glass. The facade is subdivided by steel columns 28 feet apart, clad in limestone. Because of the slightly projecting exterior support elements, a large number of the troublesome pillars could be omitted in the interior. Each of the 48 stories encompasses more than 29,000 square feet. With a gross floor area of almost 1.5 million square feet in total, the Time-Life Building was at the time of its completion the largest modernist office building. Only a few years later it would be eclipsed by the much larger International Style skyscrapers.

As a result of the New York Zoning Resolution of 1916, parts of the site of the old Roxy Theater on the west side of the building had to be purchased. On 50th Street, in addition, a further 33-foot-wide strip remained unbuilt, so that the slab-shaped office tower would take up exactly one quarter of the site's surface area. This plaza, fronting the building's south side, is paved with multicolored, undulating mosaics, which extend as far as the lobby. The entrance hall features murals by Joseph Albers and stainless-steel paneling on the outside wall of the elevator shafts.

On the east side, an azure-colored pool, edged by fountains, has been installed in front of the Time-Life Building, adjacent to William Crovello's metal sculpture *Cubed Curved* to the southeast of the site. The courtyard on the Avenue of the Americas is bordered on 51st Street by an eight-story extension, on the roof of which had long been a pavilion with dining areas and lounges. Today this area is used exclusively as office space. Since 2002 a CNN television studio has been housed in the former retail space of its lower stories. In its early years the Time-Life Building was also known especially for its club-restaurant Hemisphere Club & Tower Suite, located on the top floor. From here, between 1961 and 1971, its guests were able to enjoy a unique view of midtown Manhattan. After taller buildings began to surround it, blocking off the beautiful view, the club was closed.

XYZ BUILDINGS

ADDRESS	STORIES	COMPLETION	HEIGHT	ARCHITECT
1211–1251 AVENUE OF THE AMERICAS	45–54	1971–73	592–750 FEET	HARRISON, ABRAMOVITZ & HARRIS

The western extension of Rockefeller Center (page 150) that had begun with the Time-Life Building (page 156) was followed in the early 1970s by three additional new buildings. Because of their expressionless, almost identical character, which made them appear interchangeable, they became known as the "XYZ Buildings." They were severely criticized, and some recalled the predictions of Le Corbusier, who had foreseen the proliferation of uniformly designed skyscrapers within a highly confined space.

Each of the three office buildings was encased in a fine network of vertical supporting pillars. Because of their close proximity to one another, the facades are divided into narrow vertical units, with strip windows that are cleaned by an automatic window-washing system.

The exterior supporting framework permits extensive and column-free office levels on each floor. The three buildings escalate in height from south to north like the steps of a staircase, from the 592-foot Celanese Building to 1251 Avenue of the Americas, which stands almost 160 feet higher. As a result of the set back arrangement of the structures, extensive plazas with wide sidewalks were laid out on Avenue of the Americas. Although great effort was given regarding the design of these plazas, they remained anonymous and windswept areas that, with the exception of the lower level in front of the McGraw-Hill Building, did not meet with great public approval.

The first of the three buildings to be completed, in 1971, was the Exxon Building, which is today known by its address, 1251 Avenue of the Americas. In order to create a visual bridge to the older buildings of Rockefeller Center, its exterior supports were covered with a layer of limestone. The plaza on the Avenue of the Americas lies somewhat below street level, and features a large pool as well as the bronze sculpture *Out to Lunch*. The McGraw-Hill Building, completed shortly afterward on the south-facing site, with a gross floor area of 2.2 million square feet, is the largest of the three structures. Two-thirds of its floors are occupied by the eponymous publishing company. The exterior supports are clad in a reddish granite, which distinguishes this building from the other two.

The plaza of the McGraw-Hill Building, a few yards farther east, is indisputably the most beautifully designed forecourt of all the three buildings. The dominant element on this level is the 50-foot-high sculpture *Sun Triangle*, by Athelstan Spilhaus. Its sides correspond exactly to the angle of incidence of the sunbeams during the solstices, as well as at the spring and autumn equinoxes. On the west side of the building, behind a small extension, is a promenade for public traffic provided at the request of the city. This area is complete with a Plexiglas covered tunnel allowing visitors to walk underneath a decorative waterfall. The Celanese building, completed in 1973, is the southernmost building in the Rockefeller Center extension. Today the headquarters of Rupert Murdoch's media empire, News Corporation, it is bordered on 47th Street by a low extension, which like a boundary wall forms the southern edge of the group of buildings.

above: XYZ Buildings in the evening
left: Window cleaning gondolas on the monotone facades

W.R. GRACE BUILDING

(ALSO KNOWN AS 1114 AVENUE OF THE AMERICAS)

ADDRESS	STORIES	COMPLETION	HEIGHT	ARCHITECT
1114 AVENUE OF THE AMERICAS	50	1974	630 FEET	GORDON BUNSHAFT OF SKIDMORE, OWINGS & MERRILL

Like the Solow Building (page 147), completed the same year, the W. R. Grace Building features a base that tapers in a sloping curve to a slender high-rise slab. This design element, striking for its time, illustrated the new aims of many architects, who wanted to free themselves from the rectangular structures of the past two decades, without at the same time breaking away entirely from the principles of modernism. After the building-sector crisis in the early 1970s, a successful renaissance was hardly realized with the boxy, oversized skyscrapers whose designs only satisfied a high level of industrial utilization.

The architect of the W. R. Grace Building, Gordon Bunshaft, also had designed the Solow Building. In fact, the exterior design exactly corresponded with the original plans for the Solow Building, which were rejected by the client. While the two skyscrapers are very similar in their proportions, the profiles of their facades demonstrate significant differences. The Solow Building features a curtain wall of dark glass, while the facade of the W. R. Grace Building is distinguished by a gridlike design of white travertine and tinted window areas. Although, because of the slight setback of the tower, the continuous support struts are concealed by the row of lower buildings on 42nd Street, they still form a disturbing element in this busy pedestrian area. But on gazing up into the sky they enable spectacular perspectives, which are even enhanced by the step-free tapering of the vertical aspect of the building.

above: View from the west
below: View from Bryant Park

Despite its location in the middle of a block, the 50-story office tower is among the best-known elements on the New York skyline. This is primarily because of the unobstructed view afforded of the building's south side from opposite Bryant Park. In order to conform to zoning regulations, a wide plaza had to be created in front of the less busy north side of the building complex, which extends as far as the Avenue of the Americas. Located on the ground floor since 2005, next to a small row of stores, is an orientation center for prospective students at the City University of New York.

As a result of its tapering form, the stories of the W. R. Grace Building decrease from 40,000 square feet at ground-floor level to 25,000 square feet at the floors above the 14th story. Gordon Bunshaft deliberately chose the sloped form in order to produce a contrast with the skyscrapers of the 1920s and 1930s with their angular setbacks. It is particularly along 42nd Street that some of the best examples of the set back skyscrapers of that period are found, and accordingly the architect was subjected to harsh criticism. He responded to these reproaches with the provocative observation: "If you create a design for a skyscraper in New York which fits the context, you will later always have to deal with the problem that once the project is completed, the buildings next door have already been demolished."

500 FIFTH AVENUE

ADDRESS	STORIES	COMPLETION	HEIGHT	ARCHITECT
500 Fifth Avenue	59	1930	697 feet	Shreve, Lamb & Harmon Associates

When the foundation for the Empire State Building (page 74) was being laid, 500 Fifth Avenue, also designed by the firm of Shreve, Lamb & Harmon, was being completed only nine blocks to the north. Although this 697-foot-high office building did not yet possess the clear lines of a Daily News Building (page 92), with its reductive expression of mass, volume, and structure, it is considered a forerunner of modern high-rise architecture. The asymmetrical arrangement of its individual setbacks is the result of the building regulations for a site of only 100 x 200 feet. While on the west side the setbacks extend up to the 35th floor, forming a narrow pathway to the neighboring Salmon Tower, on the east side facing Fifth Avenue they end at the 24th floor.

The surface area of 500 Fifth Avenue is characterized by vertical window bays framed in the center by powerful supports. Particularly on the south facade it shows great similarity to that of the Empire State Building. During its early decades a large water tower stood on the roof, covered for advertising purposes with a bright red numeral "500." When the United States entered World War II, the neon tubing had to be removed because of blackout regulations. The water tower has been replaced by a somewhat unappealing cooling tower.

On its lowest four stories the building is clad in light-colored limestone, differentiating it from the brickwork of the other facade units. A gilded relief above the main entrance on Fifth Avenue depicts a woman holding a model of the building in her arms. In the lobby, clad with a lightly carved marble, a contemporary design element is represented by figures of mythical creatures. The levels above the entrance hall, particularly in the tower area, have comparatively small floor areas, so that the office tower, in spite of its 59 stories, has a gross floor area of only 600,000 square feet.

Although 500 Fifth Avenue, with its location at the intersection of Fifth Avenue and 42nd Street, stands on one of the most desirable sites in midtown Manhattan, and towers over most of the buildings that surround it, it was never able to attract the attention and prominence of other skyscrapers of its time. One of the reasons may lie in its unspectacular proportions, marked by shallow setbacks. Even the modest capital, which cannot compete with the top of the Chrysler Building (page 88) or the Chanin Building (page 84), contributes to this perception. In addition, there is no notable emphasis on any part of the building by means of symbolic decoration. For the client, however, this aspect was to play only a subordinate role, since the utilization of the building over its almost 80 years of existence has been consistently high.

above: Total view from the south
right: Entrance on Fifth Avenue

FRED F. FRENCH BUILDING

(ALSO KNOWN AS 551 FIFTH AVENUE)

ADDRESS	STORIES	COMPLETION	HEIGHT	ARCHITECT
551 Fifth Avenue	38	1927	430 feet	Sloan & Robertson, H. Douglas Ives

Two qualities distinguish the remarkable Fred F. French Building in New York's architectural history: the great variety of colors with which its many setbacks and particularly the tip of the building are decorated; and the fact that this is the first Art Deco skyscraper to culminate in a flat roof. Most of the high-rises built in the late 1920s had a slender tower ending in a stepped capital. The 19-story base of the Fred F. French building, however, is topped by a slender high-rise slab, which broke with the existing building style and was to lead the way for the later slab skyscrapers.

At a height of 430 feet, the Fred F. French Building was for a short time the tallest building on Fifth Avenue. Its unusual structure took optimal advantage of zoning regulations. On its lower 11 floors the building takes up most of the 78 x 200-square-foot site. These are followed by an eight-story unit that tapers upward in asymmetrically arranged setbacks. Colored plaster moldings are applied to its edges, which give particular emphasis to the individual setbacks. Above is a flattened shaft clad with orange-colored brick, only 26 feet wide at its narrow east and west sides. As a result of the structural division, the lower office floors, which make up the bulk of the gross floor area of 400,000 square feet, receive a sufficient supply of natural light.

The topmost unit of the building is adorned with colorful mosaics on all four sides. On the wider north and south sides, they depict a rising sun against a green background. On the left and right they are flanked by mythical creatures, which in their turn are surrounded by beehives surrounded by bees swarming. The smaller mosaics on the east and west sides portray the head of Mercury, a symbol of trade and commerce. All the motifs used embody the principles of the client, the Fred F. French company: progress, vigilance, and industry.

The lobby is also marked by elaborate detail. Its entrances on Fifth Avenue and 45th Street are framed by richly ornamented bronze-clad arches. In the entrance hall itself, in addition to the decorated bronze panels on the elevator doors, the highly adorned chandeliers are well worth seeing, hanging from a vaulted ceiling painted in warm tones. When the MetLife insurance company

above: Setbacks at the transition from the lower floors to the tower
below: The capital with its colorful mosaics and gardens

bought the building in 1985, it commissioned a comprehensive and urgently needed renovation. Along with restoration work on the lower parts of the facade, the new owners ordered a complete overhaul of the lower floor, including its 10 elevator cabs. One year later, the historical significance of the Fred F. French Building was recognized and it was granted landmark status by the New York City Landmarks Preservation Commission.

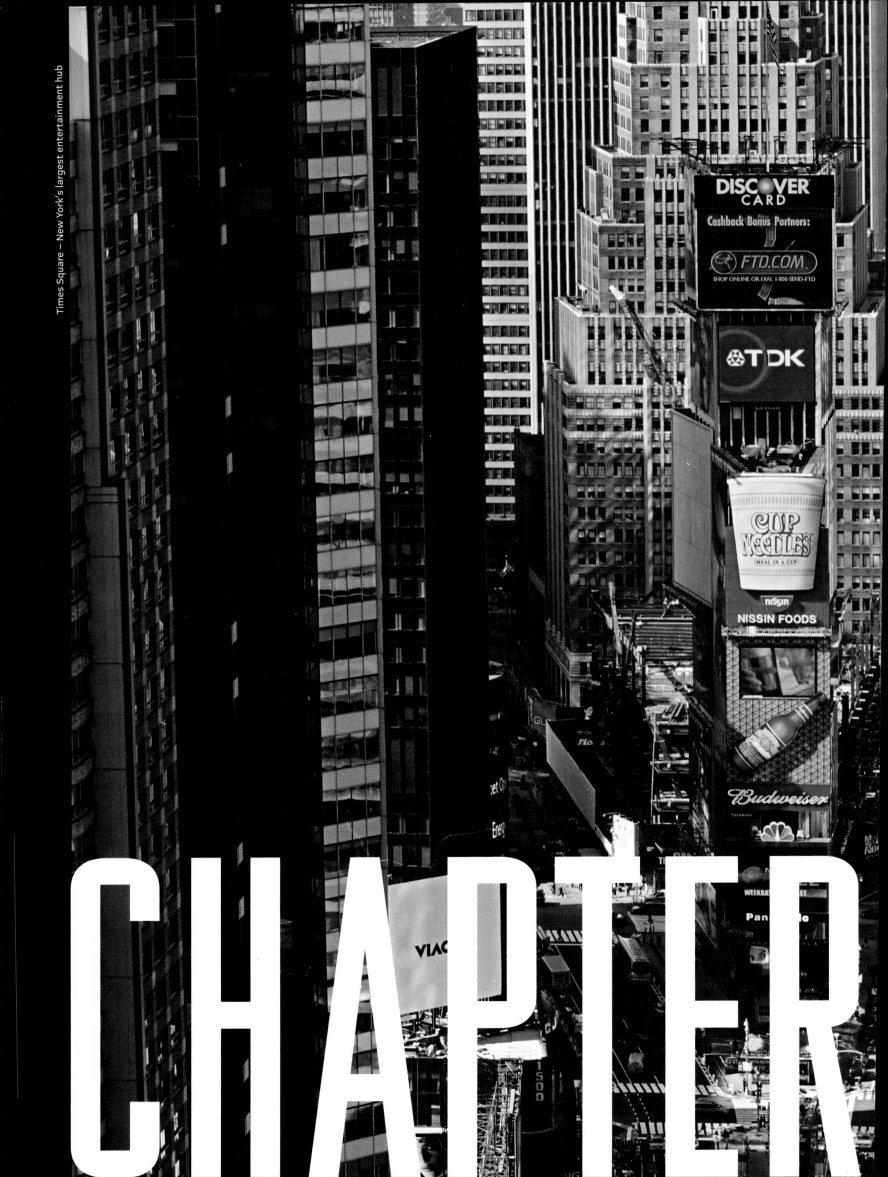

Times Square – New York's largest entertainment hub

CHAPTER

THE THEATER DISTRICT

For years, the Theater District contained only a small number of noteworthy high-rise buildings. But as a result of the continued development of Midtown West in the 1980s, a major concentration of interestingly designed skyscrapers took root. A significant number of these were completed at the zenith of postmodernism and, with their distinctive forms and wide range of colors, were easily distinguished from the monotonous buildings on the Avenue of the Americas. In the early years of the 21st century, evidence of the building boom around Times Square has continued to be felt. A several-year redevelopment plan has more than restored the area's original character as an entertainment hub. In contrast to their predecessors, these new buildings are more evolved and make use of the latest standards of technology. Of the older skyscrapers in this district, only the McGraw-Hill Building has had any decisive influence on the further development of high-rise architecture.

KEY

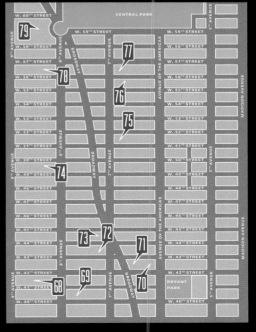

68 McGraw-Hill Building

69 New York Times Tower

70 Bank of America Tower

71 Condé Nast Building

72 Paramount Building

73 One Astor Plaza

74 One Worldwide Plaza

75 AXA Center

76 Cityspire

77 Carnegie Hall Tower

78 Hearst Tower

79 Time Warner Center

MCGRAW-HILL BUILDING

ADDRESS	STORIES	COMPLETION	HEIGHT	ARCHITECT
330 West 42ND Street	33	1931	485 FEET	RAYMOND HOOD, GODLEY & FOUILHOUX

Built in the early 1930s, the McGraw-Hill Building represents an important link in the history of skyscrapers between the streamlined Art Deco style and the functional machine aesthetic of European modernism. Raymond Hood, the architect responsible for the design, had already presented an idea of what future high-rises would look like, with his Daily News Building (page 92), a year earlier. Working with the firm of Godley & Fouilhoux, in the McGraw-Hill Building he created a combination of colorful Art Deco and simple modernist elements. Above all, however, he broke away from Louis Sullivan's emphasis on verticality.

The facades of the McGraw-Hill Building feature horizontal ribbons of windows that span the building, framed by vertical green-painted metal strips. The brick cladding was reduced in favor of larger windows, which admit a correspondingly greater amount of light to the office floors. Although the building in other respects has sternly industrial features, the facade cladding is a turquoise glazed terra-cotta brick. A few years later, at the height of modernism, typical industrial materials such as steel, concrete, and glass were being used in new buildings. With this design Hood emphasized his theory, already postulated in 1927, according to which the skyscrapers of the future could be distinctively colorful. This idea was not to be taken up to any great degree until some 50 years later, when it was embraced during the postmodernist period. In the early 1930s, the use of color was a novelty and prompted some critics to compare the building to an oversize jukebox.

In spite of its unequivocally modernist tendencies, the McGraw-Hill Building remains a typical setback skyscraper with a traditional tripartite structure. The base of the building tapers upward, after two setbacks on the north and south sides, into a high-rise slab. It terminates in a stepped flat roof, replacing the ornamental crown more frequently employed at the time. With its colorful advertising sign, the upper unit forms a recognizable landmark, visible from afar. While the McGraw-Hill Companies media conglomerate has not had its headquarters here for years, the bright red billboard shining out at night continues to make the association between the building and its former owner.

Located between Eighth and Ninth Avenues, at the time of its completion the McGraw-Hill Building stood apart from the high-rise development of midtown Manhattan. Like almost no other skyscraper before it, its structure was plainly adapted to its future tenant. While the extensive lower floors were reserved for the publishing company's printing plant, the shaft of the building was devoted to office space. At street level, the olive-green cladding was divided by gold lacquered strips of bronze. Like the frosted glass and stainless-steel ornamentation of the lobby, they typified the late Art Deco style. A year after it opened, the McGraw-Hill Building received high recognition: it was the only New York skyscraper to be included by Henry-Russell Hitchcock and Philip Johnson in the groundbreaking catalogue *The International Style,* which accompanied the Museum of Modern Art's "International Exhibition of Modern Architecture" in 1932.

above: McGraw-Hill Building with Port Authority Bus Terminal in the foreground
below: Entrance on 42nd Street

NEW YORK TIMES TOWER

(ALSO KNOWN AS NEW YORK TIMES BUILDING)

ADDRESS	STORIES	COMPLETION	HEIGHT	ARCHITECT
620 Eighth Avenue	52	2007	1,046 feet (840 feet without mast)	Fox & Fowle Architects, Renzo Piano

In the late 1990s, the New York Times Company decided to move its headquarters from its longtime location on 43rd Street to a site only a few yards south, on Eighth Avenue. In a joint venture with the developer Forest City Ratner Companies, the Times Company was to contribute to the rehabilitation of the area around the Port Authority Bus Terminal, long regarded as a blot on the cityscape. This $850-million project was part of the large-scale redevelopment of Times Square, and was supported by public funds. The city hoped that its incentive system would attract potential interested businesses and discourage the continuing migration of workplaces into parts of New Jersey. The office complex, completed in the summer of 2007, represents the third change of headquarters for the newspaper during the past century. All three locations were within four blocks of one another.

The office floors of the New York Times Tower rise in uniformly stacked layers to a height of 748 feet. Above these stories is a roof garden surrounded by maple trees, next to which is a conference center. On all four sides this level is enclosed by a framework approximately 100 feet high, which rises from a facade cladding that projects beyond the edge of the roof. A slender mast, ending at a height of 1,046 feet, grows out of the center of the roof. A low extension on the east side of the office tower accommodates a small row of stores and an inner courtyard planted with birch trees, as well as an auditorium for cultural events with seats for 350 patrons.

Unlike most examples of this generation of high-rise, the New York Times Tower has untinted window glass, which gives a transparent appearance to the structure. The unpretentiousness of this feature is part of an attempt by the Italian architect Renzo Piano, well known for his high-tech structures, to establish a link with the New York street grid and its characteristic lucid structures. In front of the greater part of the facades is a network of horizontally arranged ceramic rods, which facilitate solar and thermal protection. In order to provide an unobstructed view to office employees, however, a 35-inch-wide opening is included on each floor. Together with the glass surface, the ceramic rods ensure that the facade appears in varying color tones, depending on the exterior light conditions.

With its clear geometric proportions, the New York Times Tower dispenses with the effect-seeking features displayed by many of the new buildings in its immediate vicinity. Likewise, as a result of the increasing expansion of development westward in the early 21st century, the building's location on Eighth Avenue, once outside the boundaries of the high-rise development of midtown Manhattan, represented a decidedly smaller risk than it would have done only 10 years earlier. The economic risk could be further minimized by means of long-term contracts with the lessees. The personnel of the *New York Times*, comprising a staff of more than 2,500, occupies the lower 28 floors.

above: New York Times Tower in its urban context
left: "New York Times" logo on the facade

BANK OF AMERICA TOWER

(ALSO KNOWN AS ONE BRYANT PARK)

ADDRESS	STORIES	COMPLETION	HEIGHT	ARCHITECT
113 WEST 42ND STREET	54	2009	1,200 FEET (945 FEET WITHOUT SPIRE)	COOK + FOX ARCHITECTS

The Bank of America Tower, completed in early 2009, after a five-year building process, is among New York's most spectacular new buildings of the last 50 years. The site from which this striking office tower rises was until 2003 still marked by older buildings in dire need of renovation, whose exterior appearance no longer fit into the large-scale modernization project being undertaken along 42nd Street. The investor in the Bank of America Tower—the Durst Organization, a New York real estate firm, had become known in recent years for its environmentally conscious buildings. A joint venture with the Bank of America, the $1.3-billion project is the latest star in the revitalization of 42nd Street, which had begun 10 years earlier with the completion of the Condé Nast Building (page 174), adjacent to the west. At the same time, it also reinforced New York's claim to be the world's leading financial metropolis.

The design for the 54-story office tower is by Richard Cook. In this case, the recesses in various areas of its structure lend the building a dynamic, almost sculptural expression, which together with the transparent solid glass cladding and sharp vertical lines, create an impression of a colossal faceted crystal. Above its roof rises a centrally positioned "spire," which increases the height of the building to 1,200 feet. At this height, after the Empire State Building (page 74), it is still currently the second-tallest building in the city.

With the Bank of America Tower, the client also wanted to create a "green" workplace. Its high energy efficiency is based on a broad spectrum of installations, including rainwater collectors, water tanks within the structure of the building, recycled-heating, and a daylight-dimming system. An energy-saving wind turbine on the roof also contributes to the reduction of building-operation costs. The use of more environmentally friendly and recyclable materials, as well as more efficient integration of the outer climate by means of a special translucent glass curtain wall, enabled further highly up-to-date environmental standards to be met. The U.S. Green Building Council rated this high measure of environmentally conscious innovations accordingly, making the Bank of America Tower the first skyscraper to earn a LEED (Leadership in Energy and Environmental Design) platinum rating. The positive image this has created in the public consciousness has also affected the economic success of the building project. More than a year before its completion, all the floors already had tenants with long-term leases.

More than half of the gross floor area of 2.1 million square feet is occupied by the new New York headquarters of the Bank of

above: The building's crown during its construction phase
below: Computer rendering of the tower

America. The lower six floors at the base, with areas of up to 97,000 square feet, are ideally suited to their function as trading floors. On the west side of the base, is the renovated Henry Miller Theater, with 1,500 seats. The northeastern section of the site on the Avenue of the Americas features an enclosed green space, which is laid out as a visual extension of Bryant Park.

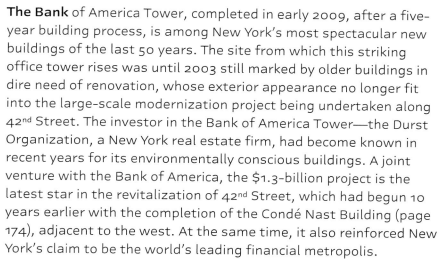

CONDÉ NAST BUILDING
(ALSO KNOWN AS 4 TIMES SQUARE)

ADDRESS	STORIES	COMPLETION	HEIGHT	ARCHITECT
4 TIMES SQUARE	48	1999	809 FEET (1,142 FEET INCL. RADIO ANTENNA)	FOX & FOWLE ARCHITECTS

When the Condé Nast Building opened its doors in 1999, it was the first major newly built skyscraper in New York for some six years. Following a recession in the building sector in the mid-1990s, its completion was one of the first signals of increased construction activity at the turn of the millennium. This 48-story office building at the same time represented the beginning of the large-scale development of the area at the intersection of Broadway and 42nd Street. In addition to the restoration of historic theaters and cinemas, the 42nd Street Development Project also provided for the creation of restaurants and shopping areas. In the meantime, with new building projects such as the Bank of America Tower (page 172), more than 6 million square feet of new office space could be created. These sometimes futuristic-looking buildings often have glass curtain-wall facades, without however lapsing into the monotony of International Style buildings.

It was not only in its external appearance, however, that the Condé Nast Building would be distinguished from the previous generation of skyscrapers. In ecological respects, too, this $500-million project invoked the latest technological developments. These include the solar panels incorporated into the facade as well as special glass that serves to reduce air-conditioning costs. All in all, energy requirements were reduced by 10 to 15 percent compared with a conventional high-rise. Apart from its own recycling system, only environmentally friendly enamels and resins were used for the furnishings.

The profile of the facade with its varied designs makes use in equal measure of classic modernist as well as postmodernist elements. This produces the impression of a conglomeration of several buildings. Each of the facades takes on the character of the immediately adjacent structures, leading to a high degree of integrity of the urban fabric. On the east and south sides, the building, otherwise surrounded by a glass curtain wall, is clad in granite, with a window grid typical of postmodernist buildings. Its double-story windows and the steel bands applied to the glass surfaces, spaced at two-story intervals, result in a halving of the scale of the building. At the intersection of Broadway and 42nd Street, the otherwise

angular building is rounded off, and on the lower floors an electronic moving message display runs over an area of some 10,800 square feet. Indicating the current NASDAQ stock prices, it terminates at the northwest corner of the building in a cylindrical visual display screen. The installation of this LED display, in its time the largest in the world, was primarily an attempt to continue the tradition of the electronic information signage on Times Square.

Not least because of the high-tech design of its spectacular roof superstructure, the Condé Nast Building is among the most striking elements on the New York skyline. On all sides, mighty structures arise, supporting a framework of 52 x 52 feet. The radio mast surmounting it was extended in October 2003 to a height of 1,142 feet, in order to replace parts of the radio broadcast system of the former World Trade Center (page 54). The fourth floor contains a cafeteria designed by the architect Frank Gehry, which is reserved for the staff of the Condé Nast magazine publishing company. The dining room, the recipient of several awards, has in its slightly raised center several seating arrangements in retro style, surrounded by large wave-shaped glass elements. At the periphery, the seating is divided into small niches by curving panels in blue titanium alloy.

above: Total view of the building at night from the north-west
below: The cafeteria designed by Frank Gehry

PARAMOUNT BUILDING

ADDRESS	STORIES	COMPLETION	HEIGHT	ARCHITECT
1501 BROADWAY	31	1927	420 FEET	RAPP & RAPP

At the turn of the 20th century, there was nothing yet to suggest that the intersection of Broadway and Seventh Avenue would one day become the unchallenged center of entertainment in New York. When the *New York Times* moved its headquarters to this area in 1904, it did so only on the condition that the square and the new subway station planned for this area should also carry the name of the newspaper. Only a few years after the completion of the Times Tower, theaters, vaudeville, and cabaret houses settled in the area, followed by restaurants and bars. To entice a well-heeled clientele, the theaters tried to draw attention by means of large advertising billboards. This tradition continues today and is a trademark of Times Square. When in the 1960s Times Square was increasingly losing its appeal, the city instituted a bonus program to encourage the building of new high-rises. Older buildings were demolished, basically modified, or repressed by massive new constructions. The Times Tower also experienced a radical redesign in the 1970s, when it was defaced on all sides with colorful neon advertising signs.

Among the few buildings on Times Square still preserved in their original form is the Paramount Building. This 31-story office building is one of the first and at the same time finest examples of the so-called "wedding cake" structures. These skyscrapers, featuring multiple setbacks due to zoning regulations at the time, were built mainly in New York in the 1920s and 1930s and presented an alternative to the existing high-rise designs, abandoning the often very striking tower finials. Each of the seven setbacks in the upper half of the building extend over only two or three stories. The capital displays on each side a clock-face 26 feet high, above which is a glass globe that increases the height of the building to 420 feet.

On its lower 12 stories, the Paramount Building takes up almost the entire site, which measures 200 x 205 feet. On its east side, facing Broadway, the building rises up another 19 stories. Above the 17th story the floors become smaller, until, on the top story, the floor area measures only 2,100 square feet. The client, the Paramount Picture Company, wanted to establish a connection between the building, the company logo and the movie business. The main facade thus takes the form of a mountain, but at the same time it also resembles a typical movie set. Its massive masonry becomes particularly striking when darkness falls and the individual setbacks are illuminated by halogen floodlights.

above: Total view of the building from the south-east
below: Times Tower

When the Paramount Building opened its doors in 1927, it was the tallest building on Times Square. Because of its conspicuous location and its unusual form, it was for many years among the best-known motifs on the New York skyline. The lower area of the building for a long time housed the Paramount Film Theater, which could seat 3,500 patrons, and where American show-business greats appeared for more than three decades. During a comprehensive renovation, the theater was closed in 1964 and transformed into additional office space. The round-arched portal over the main entrance, also removed at that time, was restored when a further reconstruction took place in the spring of 2001. With its costly decorations and projecting marquee, the entry today leads visitors into the Hard Rock Cafe, housed in the building's basement since 2005.

ONE ASTOR PLAZA
(FORMERLY W. T. GRANT BUILDING)

ADDRESS	STORIES	COMPLETION	HEIGHT	ARCHITECT
1515 Broadway	54	1972	745 feet	Der Scutt of Kahn & Jacobs

With a crown-like limestone roof featuring distinctive spike-like extensions at each of its four corners, the top of One Astor Plaza is one of the most striking on the New York skyline. The move away from a flat roof, together with the use of stone ornamentation, meant a break with the functional principles of the International style. However, the compact office tower also features a typically modernist curtain wall, which is broken up vertically by aluminum glazing bars.

This building, which covers nearly 2 million square feet, was the first to take advantage of the Special Theater District Zoning Amendment, which permitted an increase of up to 20 percent of the gross floor area for new constructions that included space for theaters, movie houses, or shopping arcades. By the 1960s, the majority of once-grand theaters in the area were antiquated and a proliferation of sex shops was accompanied by a rising crime rate. To counteract this alarming development, building regulations for the sites around Times Square were relaxed, but in order to prevent the area from being taken over by office towers, the new bonus system was instituted, intended to recapture Broadway's former vitality as an entertainment district. In the course of a few years, many other buildings would follow One Astor Plaza's example.

At street level the complex includes a small shopping center. This is connected to the upper lobby which houses the elevator shafts for the office tower that is set back about 130 feet from the Broadway sidewalks. Between 1974 and 2004, Loews Astor Plaza sat below the retail spaces. With its 1,500 seats and leopard-skin-patterned carpets, reflecting the fashion of the early 1970s, it was among the city's last big movie palaces. After a year-long conversion, it became the Nokia Theater Times Square, a live concert hall with space for more than 2,000 people. A passageway running north to south between 44th and 45th Street provides access to the Minskoff Theater on the second floor. Together with the foyer, it forms the eastern part of the base of One Astor Plaza. At the rear of the building, according to the original plans, a glazed galleria was to form a roof over the narrow Shubert Alley. Although this part of the design was not executed, the versatility of the architect Der Scutt's concept was to find wide-ranging echoes.

In its early years, One Astor Plaza still bore the name of its main tenant, the store chain W.T. Grant, whose orange logo "Grants", situated at the upper edge of the building, was visible from a distance. When this company moved out, the complex was renamed One Astor Plaza (the name comes from the Astor Hotel, which stood on this site until 1967). Today more than half the office space is occupied by the Viacom Media Company, which has its three New York MTV Studios on the first floor.

above: The distinctive roof structure
below: View from Times Square

ONE WORLDWIDE PLAZA

ADDRESS	STORIES	COMPLETION	HEIGHT	ARCHITECT
825 EIGHTH AVENUE	49	1989	778 FEET	DAVID CHILDS OF SKIDMORE, OWINGS & MERRILL

One and Two Worldwide Plaza in their urban context

The completion of One Worldwide Plaza at the end of the 1980s marked the progressing westward expansion of midtown Manhattan. Until then, Eighth Avenue was considered a sort of invisible boundary line in terms of skyscraper construction. The adjacent residential area, Hell's Kitchen, now known as Clinton, was hardly inviting at the time as a site for an impressive office tower. Despite the risks, however, after a construction period of three years, a mixed-use complex was erected on the former site of the third Madison Square Garden and is considered one of New York's most striking new buildings of the last 50 years. As a result of its modern facilities and its short distance from the Theater District, all the floors were leased within a very short time.

David Childs' design links established structures with new, extravagant forms. At first glance, One Worldwide Plaza recalls the stepped office towers, crowned with elegant capitals, of the Art Deco era. A significant difference from the skyscrapers of the late 1920s, however, is the substantially larger ground plan of the shaft—the floor area of One Worldwide Plaza measure more than 32,000 square feet. This quality also constitutes one of the great achievements of postmodernism. The buildings characterized by these stylistic elements possess the elegance and expressive power of prewar skyscrapers, without at the same time wasting unnecessary space.

The design is based on an oval, five-story platform, whose outer walls are clad with light brown granite. Its extensive levels feature five performing-arts auditoriums, as well as a small row of stores. Above this unit rises the compact shaft, which is flanked on its east and west sides by stepped 18-story extensions. The pale gray brickwork of their setbacks differentiates from the salmon-colored cladding of the rest of the building. Sturdy support struts lead to a vertical accentuation of the structure and reduce its massive effect. The seven-story unit above the 40th floor acquires an octagonal ground plan by the cutting off of its edges. Above this is a pyramidal roof extension more than 130 feet high, marked by the large openings of its ventilation installations. At dusk, a bright cone of light shines out from its glazed peak into New York's evening sky.

To the west, One Worldwide Plaza is adjacent to an open space decorated with various mosaics in stone, whose centerpiece is Sidney Simon's "Four Seasons" fountain. In recent years, small cafés and restaurants have sprung up around this square. A few yards farther west stands Two Worldwide Plaza, designed by Frank Williams & Associates. With its salmon-colored facade and crowning pyramidal roof, this 38-story apartment high-rise looks like a smaller version of its neighbor, which is twice its height.

Facade front on 49th Street

AXA CENTER

(ALSO KNOWN AS EQUITABLE CENTER TOWER WEST)

ADDRESS	STORIES	COMPLETION	HEIGHT	ARCHITECT
787 Seventh Avenue	50	1986	752 feet	Edward Larrabee Barnes Associates

When, in the early 1980s, New York was gripped by a new building boom, the centrally located sites in midtown Manhattan were already almost uniformly taken up by large office towers. Even on the Avenue of the Americas, the high-rise development was by this time extremely dense. The only option now remaining to investors was to look farther west for attractive sites. The sites on Seventh Avenue, north of 50th Street, however, were not very lucrative for major projects at this time, since the adjacent neighborhood did not enjoy a good reputation, and in addition was somewhat off the beaten track in relation to the major commercial areas.

After scouting for a new location for its headquarters, the Equitable Life Insurance Company settled on a site on Seventh Avenue between 51st and 52nd Street. The insurance company already owned the site west of the adjacent headquarters. To carry out this rather risky project, Equitable Life entered into a partnership with the real estate company Tishman Speyer Properties. In order to make the new office building even more attractive to prospective tenants, it had to offer not only modern facilities but additional amenities as well. Among these amenities are the AXA Gallery with its diverse artworks, an auditorium, and the company's fitness center, next to which is a large swimming pool. Ease of travel was ensured by the proximity of several subway stations.

Edward Larrabee Barnes was responsible for the design of the 752-foot skyscraper. It was particularly important to his clients that the base of the building be striking and stand out from its surroundings. Barnes created an impressive entrance area, among the most beautiful in New York. The visual highlight of the six-story atrium, accentuated by the round arches of its mighty portals, is Roy Lichtenstein's *Mural with Blue Brushstroke*. The painted mural, measuring 72 x 36 feet, is a collage of earlier works by the renowned New York-based Pop artist. In order to create the painting within the short time frame of six weeks, Lichtenstein used slide projectors to aid him in sketching the surfaces. With additional artworks and a variety of exhibitions held in the AXA Gallery, where admission is free, the insurance company also emphasized its leading role as an insurer of art.

The facade profile of the AXA Center has a gridlike design, which results from the vertical strut supports clad in red-brown granite and horizontal white parapet bands. The double-story uppermost floor has a large round-arched window on each of the east and west sides, behind which are exclusive banquet facilities. Soon after the 50-story office building was completed, it was joined by many other new structures along Seventh Avenue. At the same time, the neighboring older buildings appeared in new glory after extensive restoration work. As a result of these developments, the area known as Midtown West gained a new cachet that it still retains today.

above: View from the south-west
below: Atrium featuring a painting by Roy Lichtenstein

CITYSPIRE

ADDRESS	STORIES	COMPLETION	HEIGHT	ARCHITECT
156 West 56th Street	72	1989	814 feet	Murphy/Jahn Inc. Architects

Cityspire, Carnegie Hall Tower (page 185), and Metropolitan Tower are three immense skyscrapers that were built in the late 1980s within a tightly confined space between 56th and 57th Street. Each of the buildings contains 60 or more stories and all have become dominant elements on Seventh Avenue. Their dizzying heights and the close spacing between the structures constitute forceful reminders of the narrow canyons of streets in the Financial District. The tallest of these quite differently designed buildings is Helmut Jahn's Cityspire. This mixed-use 72-story structure is among the generation of high-rises—built with increasing frequency in recent years— that are supported by concrete frames. As a result of continuing improvements in quality (the high-performance concrete used has a pressure resistance three times greater than traditional concrete), buildings with this support system, instead of a steel skeleton, could now be constructed beyond the 700-foot limit.

The central tower element has an octagonal ground plan. On the east and west it is flanked by two extensions, which end, after two narrowing setbacks, at the level of the 60th floor. The structure's tapering form and the continuous window bars give the building a strikingly vertical accentuation. This upward-aspiring character can be best understood from the vantage point of the sidewalks on 55th and 56th Street, from which the streamlined skyscraper seems to grow almost endlessly into the sky.

The capital consists of a stepped, three-story unit that is enclosed by a copper-clad dome. With this crown-like finial, Helmut Jahn makes an effective allusion to the domed roof of the City Center for the Performing Arts, adjacent to the south. By transferring its air rights, this building of 1924 made it possible for Cityspire to be realized at its present height. Its gross floor area of 830,000 square feet is still comparatively small considering its height and number of stories.

View from the south-east

As with almost all mixed-use skyscrapers, the 23 office floors of Cityspire are accommodated in the lower part of the building and have a separate entrance. Above the 24th floor, which houses the building's fitness center, are 339 apartments. With the increasing height of the structure, the living space rises to an area of some 2,200 square feet on the upper floors. During severe storms, however, the residents of these stories suffer from the clearly audible vibration of the building, which results from the slender form of the tower.

Facade front on 56th Street

CARNEGIE HALL TOWER

ADDRESS	STORIES	COMPLETION	HEIGHT	ARCHITECT
152 West 57th Street	60	1990	757 feet	Cesar Pelli & Associates

Carnegie Hall, opened in 1891, was New York's first great concert hall. In addition to its splendid interior decoration— which, with its bronze balconies and ornamental stucco work, can compare with the famous European concert houses—its outstanding acoustics, especially, guarantee its continuing status as one of the most famous and sought-after music venues in the world. In order to finance an urgently needed restoration, in the 1980s the Carnegie Hall directors decided to sell part of the site and transfer the building's air rights to a new skyscraper to be erected here. The American architect Cesar Pelli was commissioned to design Carnegie Hall Tower. Pelli, who was born in Argentina and had lived in the United States since 1952, had already proved his skill in this respect with his design for Museum Tower (page 148), part of the expansion of the Museum of Modern Art.

The neo-Renaissance-style Carnegie Hall Tower was designed to harmonize perfectly with the famous concert hall. Pelli combined the simplicity of the rectangular form with a lavish facade design. To give the 60-story structure a contextual exterior, he used an orange-brown-colored brick cladding for the facade material. The result is a building that differentiates itself pleasingly from many of its contemporaries. With its extremely slender slab form, it is more reminiscent of a prewar skyscraper than akin to the postmodernist high-rises with their larger ground plans. Also, in its coloration, Carnegie Hall Tower competes favorably with the key buildings of the late 1920s.

Two years before the completion of Carnegie Hall Tower, the 68-story Metropolitan Tower was erected on the site immediately adjacent to the east. Its facades, unlike those of its neighbor, are clad entirely in reflective glass. Above the 18th floor the building acquires a triangular plan, which converges at 57th Street in a very sharp point. Because of their differing designs and ground plans, these skyscrapers, separated from each other by only 20 feet, form some of the most tension-filled counterparts on the New York skyline.

above: Carnegie Hall Tower with Metropolitan Tower (left)
right: Total view of the building
left: Roof gardens on the west side of the tower

HEARST TOWER

(ALSO KNOWN AS HEARST MAGAZINE TOWER)

ADDRESS	STORIES	COMPLETION	HEIGHT	ARCHITECT
300 WEST 57TH STREET	42	2006	597 FEET	FOSTER & PARTNERS

Hearst Tower, opened in the summer of 2006, bears the unmistakable handwriting of its architect, Norman Foster. In his first design for a New York high-rise, Foster decided on a glass-clad steel skeleton construction, whose supports run at a 65-degree angle, lending the facade a diamond-shaped pattern. As a result of their particular arrangement, the supporting elements diminish the gravitational and lateral forces, so that the structure acquires stability without additional strengthening or concrete walls. The result is a reduction of the steel tonnage by 20 percent compared with a conventionally constructed office building with a rectangular support system.

The new headquarters of the Hearst Corporation, the venerable communications media company, were built above the Hearst Magazine Building erected in 1928. In the original plans, this six-story building was already intended to be only the basis for a high-rise to be constructed at a future date. Following the Great Depression, however, the additional building plans were put on hold indefinitely and did not begin to take shape again until the end of the 20th century. A striking presence, Hearst Tower has contributed significantly to increasing the appeal of the Columbus Circle area in recent years.

The 42-story office tower rests on its own foundations, without detracting from the structural elements and facades of the old building, which has been landmarked since 1988. The base of the new tower has been designed to be integrated into the center of the Hearst Magazine Building. Escalators flanked by waterfalls lead employees into an impressive atrium. This 80-foot-high space, dominated by massive stainless-steel supports, forms a seamless link with the tower rising above it. Also located here, in addition to the fastest elevators in New York, is Cafe 57, as well as an exhibition space devoted to the Hearst Corporation. The overriding feature, however, is the contrast between the limestone walls of the old building and the 21st-century architecture that rises above it.

With the Hearst Tower, Norman Foster was once again able to demonstrate his exceptional gift for making use of energy-efficient designs. The British architect, who was awarded the Pritzker Prize in 1999, had already caused a sensation in the 1980s with his design for the headquarters of the Hong Kong and Shanghai Banking Corporation in Hong Kong. Although many of the more recently built New York skyscrapers have also incorporated improved energy efficiency, the Hearst Tower, together with the new Seven World Trade Center (page 57), was the first New York office tower to earn

above: Entrance to the atrium on Eighth Avenue
below: Decorative columns accent the corners of the old Hearst Magazine Building

a LEED (Leadership in Energy and Environmental Design) gold rating from the U.S. Green Building Council for energy conservation and environmentally conscious design. Contributing to the building's sustainability, in addition to the energy-saving glazing, are the efficient heating and ventilating system, the use of rainwater for irrigation and cooling, and measuring devices to reduce lighting costs. Through these measures, the Hearst Tower has been able to reduce its operating costs by 25 percent compared with a conventional office high-rise. The other side of the coin, however, is the significant increase in building costs. In relation to its gross floor area of 860,000 square feet, this $500-million project is among the most expensive office buildings in the world.

TIME WARNER CENTER

ADDRESS	STORIES	COMPLETION	HEIGHT	ARCHITECT
10 Columbus Circle	55	2004	750 feet	David Childs of Skidmore, Owings & Merrill

In the spring of 2004 the largest new building project in New York for many years was completed on the former site of the New York Coliseum. Together with smaller projects, the Time Warner Center is part of an extensive redevelopment of the area around Columbus Circle. The $1.7-billion complex has a gross floor area of 2.5 million square feet and, as a result of its dimensions and varied uses, extends to six separate addresses. With an area of 915,000 square feet, the glass surface is the size of more than 10 soccer fields.

The design by David Childs specifies a large-scale base that covers almost the entire site. His east facade is concave and follows the contours of the neighboring traffic circle. On the north and south sides rise two tower extensions clad in blue-colored glass, which engage in intimate dialogue with the double-towered apartment buildings on the west side of Central Park. At a height of 750 feet, they are, since the destruction of the World Trade Center (page 54), the city's tallest twin towers. Their shafts, with graduated setbacks in the lowest third of the building, terminate in a slightly stepped capital.

About one-third of the total effective area is taken up by Time Warner Inc., the largest media conglomerate in the world, which has its headquarters here, in addition to several television studios. The north tower houses, among other spaces, the Mandarin Oriental Hotel New York. Occupying an area of 270,000 square feet, this five-star hotel contains 250 luxuriously furnished bedrooms, spacious suites, and a ballroom for 500 guests. Above the spa on the 35th floor is the hotel's glassed-in swimming pool, from which guests can enjoy a splendid view as far as the Hudson River. The Time Warner Center complex also includes Jazz at Lincoln Center, a concert facility with a 1,100-seat auditorium and its own recording studios, as well as six office floors and more than 200 apartments. The 13,000-square-foot penthouse apartment achieved the possibly record-breaking sales price of $45 million.

In contrast to the concrete-framed towers, the base has a steel frame structure. At the so-called Palladium at Time Warner Center, a five-story shopping arcade, more than 50 stores, six restaurants, and a large health club are installed in an area of 355,000 square feet. The main entrance is formed by a glass frontage 130 feet high and 85 feet wide, which is subdivided by narrow metal bands. Adjoining this is a 100-foot-tall atrium, whose elevators and escalators lead visitors to the individual floors of the shopping arcade. The escalator in the center of the entrance hall leads to the underground levels. In addition to a large supermarket, these accommodate a three-story parking garage with 500 parking spaces and the center's direct subway entrance.

above: View from Central Park
left: "Palladium at Time Warner Center"

GLOSSARY

Arcade: An archway supported by pillars or columns, or a row of arches.

Art Deco: Elegant, streamlined architectural style, whose name is derived from the Paris exhibition "Exposition Internationale des Arts Décoratifs et Industriels Modernes." In the late 1920s, Art Deco skyscrapers, characterized by geometric designs and the use of materials such as stainless steel, aluminum and inlaid wood, formed the transition from neoclassicism to European modernism.

Beaux-Arts style: Architectural style named after the Ecole des Beaux-Arts in Paris, in which buildings frequently combine elements of diverse historical styles and make use of artistic, sometimes even flamboyant expression.

Chicago School: First significant style in high-rise building, which originated in Chicago in the late 19th century. Architects in the circle of Louis Sullivan aimed at structural forms and functional designs. The most prominent characteristic of these buildings was an emphasis on the vertical, a tripartite facade composition, and a concluding flat roof.

Colonnade: Arcade with straight entablature, as opposed to one surmounted by arches.

Curtain wall: A glass "curtain" without a supportive function, placed in front of the framework of a modernist skyscraper. In combination with rust-free steel frames, the windows form a smooth facade surface, behind which are the support elements. The curtain wall is one of the most striking features of modernist architecture.

Gross floor (surface) area: This is the sum of all individual floor areas, calculated by measuring the overall dimensions of each floor. Unlike the net area or usable living area, this concept includes all the walls.

International Style: The American term for the Bauhaus style of European modernism.

Modernism: Modernism is an important style of the 20th century, based on the principles of functionalism and the standardized, rectangular metal and glass structures of the Bauhaus. It developed from the attempt to free structural form from the historical elements that concealed it. The idea of the unity of mind and matter rested on the principle that the building should be the simplified expression of its materials and ground plans.

Neoclassicism: General term for artistic styles that consciously refer to models from classical antiquity. In high-rise buildings in New York in the early 20th century, neoclassicism was strongly influenced by the Ecole des Beaux-Arts.

New York City Landmarks Preservation Commission: A New York City group founded in 1965, which officially grants landmark status to buildings that are of exceptional significance in urban planning history or have special aesthetic value. A building must have been existed for 30 years before it can be considered for landmark status.

New York Zoning resolution of 1916: This legislation restricted the ways in which the areas of skyscrapers could be structured, allowing more natural daylight to enter Manhattan's street canyons. The skyscrapers built during the validity of this law often included stepped setbacks near the base and usually culminated in a slender tower.

New York Zoning resolution of 1961: The 1961 zoning resolution replaced that of 1916, making the gross floor area of a building dependent on the size of the site. By simultaneously making public spaces available, the factor could be increased up to 20 percent. In addition the law enabled the purchase and transfer of air rights.

Postmodernist architecture: In the late 1970s, postmodernism marked a break with the functional and uniform structures of modernism. In contrast to the latter, postmodernism is based on the principle of heterogeneity. Its buildings represent a juxtaposition of the diverse stylistic eras and demonstrate a strong affinity for design, but it rejects thoughtless imitation of historical models.

Setback skyscrapers: This type of skyscraper, frequently built in New York, represented the logical consequence of the New York Zoning Resolution of 1916. In conformity with the building regulations, buildings were "set back" in graduated steps until the floor area covered only a quarter of the site. Often the buildings were given a slender, centrally positioned tower extension.

U.S. Green Building Council: Nonprofit U.S.-based organization and testing center for environmentally friendly and energy-efficient building construction. The buildings are rated based on their environmental friendliness according to the evaluation system called "Leadership in Energy and Environmental Design" (LEED). The standards are defined in the following categories: location concept, water and energy utilization, materials, and sustainable interior construction.

INDEX OF PROPER NAMES

PHOTOGRAPHIC CREDITS

Jörg Machirus: photographs on pages: 7, 8, 9 (below), 10, 12, 13 (below), 14, 18, 19, 20, 21 (below), 21, 22, 23 (below), 24, 25, 26, 27, 28 (center, below), 29, 31, 32, 33, 34, 35, 37, 38, 39 (above), 40, 41 (below), 44, 45, 47, 48, 49, 50, 51, 52 (below), 53, 56 (below), 57, 58, 59 (above), 60, 61, 62, 66, 67, 68, 69, 70, 73, 75, 76 (above, center), 77, 78, 79 (below), 80, 81, 82 (center, below), 83 (below), 84, 85, 86, 89 (center, below), 91, 92, 93, 95, 96 (below), 97, 98, 99, 100, 101, 102, 103, 104, 105, 106, 107, 108 (above), 110, 111 (above), 112, 114, 116, 117, 118, 119, 120, 121 (above), 122, 123,124, 127, 128, 130, 131 (below), 132, 133, 134, 136, 137 (below), 138, 139 (above)142, 143 (above), 144 (below), 145, 146, 147, 148 (below), 149 (above), 150,151, 152 (left), 152, 153 (above left, above right), 154, 155, 156, 157, 158, 160 (above),162, 163 (below), 165, 166, 168, 169 (above), 170, 171, 174, 175 (above), 176, 177 (below), 178, 179, 180, 181, 182, 183, 184, 185 (below right), 186, 187, 188, 189

Scott Murphy: photographs on pages: 4/5, 11 (above), 13 (above), 16, 21 (above), 23 (above), 28 (above), 30, 36, 39 (below), 41 (above), 42, 46, 52 (above), 54, 56 (above), 59 (below), 63 (below), 64, 71, 72, 74, 76 (below), 79 (above), 82 (above), 83 (above), 88, 89 (above, below), 90, 94, 96 (above), 108 (below), 109, 111 (below), 115, 121 (below), 125 (above), 126, 129, 131 (above), 135, 137 (above), 140, 144 (above), 148 (above), 149 (below right, below left), 153 (above center, below), 153 (below), 159, 160 (below), 161, 163 (above), 164, 172, 173 (above), 177 (above), 185 (above, below left)

Dirk Stichweh: photographs on pages: 143 (below), 169 (below) street maps of New York: pages: 17, 43, 65, 87, 13, 141, 167

Archiv Simmen / Drepper, Berlin: photograph on page: 6 (below)
dpa-picture-alliance: photographs on pages: 4, 6 (above), 9 (above), 11 (below), 55 (above and below), 63 (below), 125 (below), 139 (below)
Cook + Fox Architects, New York / dBox for Cook + Fox Architects : rendering on page: 173 (below)
Roger Dong '2000 and Condé Nast Publications: photograph on page: 175 (below)
laif, Cologne: Langrock / Zenit: photograph on page: 15 (above)
Skidmore, Owings & Merrill LLP: photograph on page: 15 (below)

AUTHOR'S ACKNOWLEDGEMENTS

This book would not have been possible without the friendly support of many persons to whom I am greatly indebted. First of all, I would like to thank the photographers Jörg Machirus and Scott Murphy, with whom I had the pleasure of spending many wonderful and exiting days on my visits to New York. For factual questions regarding architecture, I was able to rely on architect Thomas Klumpp from Bremen. Alexandra Meyder-Cyrus from the Deutsche Bank Real Estate in New York, through her good contacts, was able to facilitate our entrance into many buildings. My thanks also go out to Jürgen Krieger, Katharina Haderer, Curt Holtz, and Reegan Köster at Prestel Publishing. However, the most important support and motivation throughout this project was that from my wife Petra and our son Robin, to whom I would like to dedicate this book.

I am also indebted to the following persons and institutions:
Gaston Silva, Kathy Chou, Justine M. Urbaites – Vornado Realty Trust, New York
Tim Clancy, Peter Karas – Durst Organization, New York
Tom Hardardt, Walter Maher, Mike Ferraro, Perry Incantalupo – Craven Corporation, New York
Thomas Chiodo, Yonit Golub, Iva Benson – Rubenstein Communications, New York
Stefan Brendgen – Tishman Speyer Properties, Frankfurt
Roy Suskin – Property Manager Woolworth Building, New York
Leslie Lefkowitz – Director of Public Relations, Four Seasons Hotel, New York
John T. Henriques – Property Manager Trump World Tower, New York
Jack Lieb – Chief Engineer Tower 49, New York
Barry Mann – General Manager New Yorker Hotel, New York
Drew Masters, Robert J. McKeown – Hines Real Estate, New York
Deutsche UN-Vertretung, New York
Courtney Long, Lou Hammond & Associates
Matthew Cherry, Edward Hogan, Brookfield Properties
MaryAnne Gilmartin, Julie Hendricks, Forest City Ratner Companies
Kacey Kennedy, Trump Organization
Kathy Baquerizo, DB Real Estate New York
Melissa Libner, Melanie Pimentel, SL Green Realty Corporation
Bob Bennis, Conde Nast Publication
Ariel Jordan, Time Warner Inc.
Anja Cordes, Michael Heyder – editorial
and to the many citizens of New York City, who time and time again were of great assistance to me and my work.

Front cover: Two New York Icons, the Empire State Building and the Chrysler Building. Photograph by Jörg Machirus
Back cover: The Chrysler Building in the evening hours. Photograph by Scott Murphy
Page 2: Manhattan Island, from Battery Park looking north. Photograph by Scott Murphy
Backflap-Photographs by Jörg Machirus (above, below) and Dirk Stichweh (center)

Prestel Verlag
Königinstrasse 9
80539 Munich
Tel. +49 (0)89 24 29 08-300
Fax +49 (0)89 24 29 08-335

Prestel Publishing Ltd.
4 Bloomsbury Place
London WC1A 2QA
Tel. +44 (0)20 7323-5004
Fax +44 (0)20 7636-8004

Prestel Publishing
900 Broadway, Suite 603
New York, N.Y. 10003
Tel. +1 (212) 995-2720
Fax +1 (212) 995-2733

www.prestel.com

Prestel books are available worldwide. Please contact your nearest bookseller or one of the above addresses for information concerning your local distributor.

The Library of Congress Control Number: 2008942990
British Library Cataloguing-in-Publication Data: a catalogue record for this book is available from the British Library. The Deutsche Bibliothek holds a record of this publication in the Deutsche Nationalbibliografie; detailed bibliographical data can be found under: http://dnb.ddb.de

Translated from German by: Paul Aston (forword, essay, Chapter 1, and Chapter 2), John Sykes, Cologne (Chapter 3), Ian Pepper, Berlin (Chapter 4 and Chapter 5), Christine Shuttleworth, London (Chapter 6, Chapter 7, and appendix)

Editorial direction by Curt Holtz & Reegan Köster
Copyediting by Stephanie Solomon, New York
Design by Liquid, Augsburg
Production by Sebastian Runow
Layout by Andrea Mogwitz, Munich
Origination by ReproLine mediateam, Munich
Printed and bound by TBB, Banská Bystrica

Printed in Slovakia on acid-free paper

ISBN 978-3-7913-4054-8

LONGWOOD PUBLIC LIBRARY
800 Middle Country Road
Middle Island, NY 11953
(631) 924-6400
mylpl.net

LIBRARY HOURS

Monday-Friday	9:30 a.m. - 9:00 p.m.
Saturday	9:30 a.m. - 5:00 p.m.
Sunday (Sept-June)	1:00 p.m. - 5:00 p.m.